THE BLACK HOLE OF
CALCUTTA

THE BLACK HOLE
OF CALCUTTA

A Reconstruction

by

Noel Barber

A COMMON READER EDITION
The Akadine Press

The Black Hole of Calcutta

A COMMON READER EDITION published 2000 by
The Akadine Press, Inc., by arrangement with The Estate of Noel Barber.

A COMMON READER EDITION and fountain colophon
are trademarks of The Akadine Press, Inc.

ISBN 1-58579-007-9

10 9 8 7 6 5 4 3 2 1

This book is for
TITINA

'The capture of Fort William, and the sufferings of its inhabitants, strongly evince the fallacy of all human speculations. For nearly a century, it had been the constant object of the East India Company to procure a fortification on the Ganges for the protection of their servants and property: had they never obtained it, the catastrophe would not have happened. On the other hand, the Nabob supposed that, from the capture of the Fort, and the destruction of the garrison, he had rendered his government secure, and expelled the English from the country: whereas that very circumstance drew on him the vengeance of an inveterate foe, caused his death, and transferred the government to the hands of strangers.'

Charles Stewart in
A History of Bengal (1813)

Contents

Acknowledgements

My thanks are due to the Commonwealth Relations Office Library for their valued assistance in searching out original documents relating to the East India Company. Official correspondence written at the time of the Black Hole is still in the Library's possession and they were able to make available to me hundreds of documents, minutes of proceedings and reports to the Court of Directors without which this book could never have been written.

The panoramic view of Calcutta is reproduced by kind permission of the Dorset Military Museum, and the portrait of Holwell by kind permission of the India Office Print Library.

I am most grateful to Donald Dinsley who for two years unflaggingly co-ordinated all the research, and to Miss Ann Stoneham who typed out several versions of the manuscript before the final copy evolved.

Lastly I wish to thank James Kinross the novelist, a close and staunch friend, who painstakingly helped and advised me with the manuscript from the very first page to the last.

Cast of Principal Characters

CIVILIANS

Members of Council

ROGER DRAKE, *President and Governor*
JOHN ZEPHANIAH HOLWELL, *Senior Magistrate*
CHARLES MANNINGHAM, *Export Warehouse Keeper*
WILLIAM FRANKLAND, *Import Warehouse Keeper*
WILLIAM WATTS, *Chief of Cossimbazaar Station*
WILLIAM MACKETT, *Paymaster*

Factors

JOHN O'HARA, *Engineer*
WILLIAM TOOKE, *an Accountant*

Writers

HENRY LUSHINGTON
RALPH THORESBY
ROBERT WILKINSON

Unclassified

THE REV. GERVAS BELLAMY, *Chaplain*
DOROTHY, *his wife*
ANNA, *his daughter*
THOMAS, *his elder son*
THE REV. ROBERT MAPLETOFT, *Assistant Chaplain*
SARAH, *his wife*
LADY RUSSELL, *a widow*
PETER CAREY, *a seafaring man*
MARY, *his half-caste wife*

CAST OF PRINCIPAL CHARACTERS

WILLIAM GRAY, *Surgeon*
JANNIKO, *a fiddler*
THOMAS LEACH, *Carpenter*
ANNE MACKETT, *wife of a Council Member*

MILITARY

CAPT.-COMMANDANT GEORGE MINCHIN, *Garrison Commander*
CAPT. DAVID CLAYTON, *Second-in-Command*
CAPT. ALEXANDER GRANT, *Adjutant-General*
CAPT. LAWRENCE WITHERINGTON, *of Garrison powder store*
LIEUT. JOHN BELLAMY, *the Chaplain's younger son*
LIEUT. THOMAS BLAGG
LIEUT. MELCHIOR LEBEAUME, *a deserter from the French*
LIEUT. WILLIAM BAILLIE, *Military Storekeeper*
ENSIGN CHARLES SMITH
ENSIGN PETER CARSTAIRS
ENSIGN JOHN FRANCIS PICCARD
SERGEANT HEDLEBURGH, *a Dutch mercenary*

Sea Captains

CAPTAIN ANDREW YOUNG, *of the 'Dodaldy'*
CAPTAIN JOHN MILLS, *of the 'Diligence'*
CAPTAIN THOMAS HAGUE, *of the 'Prince George'*

THE OPPOSITE CAMP

SIRAJ-UDDAULA, *the Nabob of Bengal*
ROY DOOLUB, *his troop Commander*
THE MARQUIS DE ST JACQUES, *a renegade Frenchman in charge of the Nabob's artillery*
KISSENDASS, *the Nabob's cousin*
OMICHAND, *a Jain merchant*
JAGGERNATH SINGH, *Omichand's servant*

Author's Note

Every schoolboy knows about the Black Hole of Calcutta, or believes he does, for it appears in the history
curriculum as regularly as the Battle of Hastings or the
South Sea Bubble. Yet it is surprising how little most
people know about the siege which preceded this melancholy event; a four-day battle of astonishing ferocity in
which a garrison of five hundred and fifteen Europeans
fought desperately against an overwhelming force of
fifty thousand Indians.

Here is something vastly more dramatic than a mere
chronicle of day-to-day fighting. Here is a story in
which the humid, enervating heat of Calcutta, the
primitive conditions, the fearful disparity in numbers, the
inner knowledge that the catastrophe could easily have
been averted, combined to bring out the very best and
very worst qualities in the diverse, polyglot and doomed
garrison.

A novelist could hardly assemble a cast more richly
endowed with human strengths and weaknesses than the
men and women who actually took part in and even survived this moment of history two hundred years ago—
a moment in which a handful of Englishmen, many of
them youngsters, were callously deserted by their leaders
and then, as they fought on, were betrayed.

I have called this volume a Reconstruction because I

have taken certain liberties in writing it. I do not see how they can offend the more orthodox historian, for in my experience human beings react today very much as they did two hundred years ago, and any techniques I have employed to clothe the sometimes dry bones of history with colour and life in no way interfere with the historically important facts.

Here, then, is the garrison of Calcutta. Some lived through the Black Hole, some died, some deserted before that terrible night. Some were astonishingly brave, others were cowards. A few were astute, others were stupid to the point of exasperation. The fates of all the characters involved in the hideous nightmare have been faithfully recorded, together with each step leading to the night in the Black Hole.

I have taken the further liberty of eliminating several characters who contributed nothing to the final result and whose actions would have only impeded the story. It seemed in the best interests of smooth narrative to do this. In contrast I have expanded some of the others, basing my portrayal of their characters on their recorded actions.

I was faced with another minor problem. In one or two unimportant incidents which are known to have occurred, the exact time is a matter of conjecture. We are told, for example, that the chaplain's eldest son shot himself on the walls, that one wife bore a daughter 'during the troubles', that another had a miscarriage. But though there is a precise historical timetable covering the military action, we are never told exactly when incidents of this nature occurred. I have allowed them to enter the story where they seemed to fall most naturally.

This does not mean, however, that I have tampered with history. For this is in no sense 'a romantic novel based on the incident of the Black Hole'. It is a true story; its characters live and die as they lived and died two hundred years ago.

One other point should be mentioned. From time to time small pamphlets have appeared suggesting that the night of the Black Hole never occurred, that it is a legend perpetrated by the British to excuse the dominion over India which followed as a direct result of the fall of Calcutta.

I have ignored all such suggestions, for there seems to me irrefutable proof that the event occurred. All too often claims such as these are ill-informed and, one suspects, motivated by reasons other than a search for historical accuracy.

I have particularly in mind a book entitled *The Myth of the Britannica* in which the American Dr Harvey Einbinder, in seeking to discredit that remarkable work of reference, launched a ridiculous attack on the *Britannica's* account of the Black Hole. This is hardly the place to enter into an argument, but there is perhaps one point worth making. Invariably, one curious omission marks the arguments of those who claim the night of the Black Hole never occurred: if the one hundred and twenty-three British prisoners did not die in the Black Hole, where did they die? It is inconceivable that the standard three-volume reference work on this period of British history (*Bengal in 1756-57* by C. R. Hill), which contains over a thousand pages of documentary evidence and verbatim testimony by survivors of the Black Hole, should ignore the fate of these men when the fates of all the others are carefully recorded.

John Zephaniah Holwell, who commanded the Fort after the Governor deserted and lived through the Black Hole, described the night with such a wealth of detail that one is apt to forget that his record was confirmed by at least two others who lived through that terrible night.

For instance, there was Captain Mills of the garrison who kept a small diary in which he wrote: 'most of those that remained were put into the Black Hole to the number of 144 . . . of whom upwards of one hundred and twenty were miserably smothered by the heat occasioned by so many being shut up in so small a place, as to be obliged to stand upon one another.'

Another witness, John Cooke, Secretary to the Governor, also lived through the night of the Black Hole, and in his evidence under oath at the committee of enquiry, stated categorically: 'a party of fellows came and ordered us to walk into the place before mentioned called the Black Hole, a room or rather dungeon, about eighteen feet long and fourteen feet wide, with only two air holes . . . Into this hole we were forcibly crammed about eight o'clock in the evening, and the door immediately locked upon us. The number of souls thrust into this dungeon was near one hundred and fifty, among which was one woman and twelve of the wounded officers . . . and when we were released, at six o'clock the next morning, only twenty-two came out alive.'

Such statements make nonsense of attacks by men such as Einbinder who chose not to include them, and in fact only use the episode of the Black Hole as part of an overt attack on something else.

I find it impossible to believe that Holwell, a surgeon and a lawyer, would dare (as some suggest) to invent an episode that never took place and then name twenty-three survivors who were supposed to have passed the night with him. If Holwell invented the story, how was it that not one of the twenty-three persons he names denied the story when evidence of the fall of Calcutta was being taken?

This, then, is the story as I know it. I have lived with it now for two years until its characters have become my waking acquaintances and the fate of the garrison as real and as vivid as if this episode of history occurred yesterday instead of two hundred years ago.

I am very much aware that despite my own strongly-held beliefs, there are some who may not agree with all my conclusions. One cannot hope to please everybody and even after two hundred years the facts which are incontrovertible still give rise to argument.

I do not pretend that this book is a definitive work. What I have set out to do is to write for the general reader a narrative account of an extraordinary event which had violent and lasting repercussions.

CHAPTER ONE

The Years of Discontent

Before Saturday, June 5, 1756

In the last uneasy days before decades of peaceful, un-hurried existence were to be shattered, those who were afraid still clung to one hope. If their worst fears were realized, if the Nabob marched, there was always the Fort. Crouching in the heart of the city, its bulk dominating the Hoogly river, its grey mass presented a challenge no invader could ignore. It was over seven hundred feet long; its north face measured three hundred and ten feet, while the south curtain stretched for nearly five hundred feet. With ten cannon mounted on each of its four corner bastions, the Fort represented some-thing more than a stern deterrent to the native popula-tion or suspicious ships on the Hoogly river. It was the heart and soul of Calcutta. Men lived in Fort William, worked in this town within a town. It was, in the minds of the inhabitants, impregnable. No matter what hap-pened, every one of the five hundred British men, women and children in Calcutta believed they could withstand a siege for days, weeks, months, sheltered behind its high walls and cannon. And even if the impossible happened, if sickness or some unsuspected tragedy reduced the garrison to a state where it could defend those walls no longer, then in the last resort there would always be a secure line of retreat by the river, where, in those last hot, still weeks before the attack, nearly twenty stout British vessels lay at anchor.

To the men and women of Calcutta whose secure, if isolated, lives had been rudely interrupted by rumours of trouble with the Moors (as the Moslem rulers of Bengal were known), Fort William must have seemed as secure as the East India Company for which they worked—as solid as England itself, for that was what it represented: a corner of England constructed by English ingenuity in an alien land, built to withstand any attack the heathens dared to launch.   A symbol of defiance, perhaps, but more than that: a guarantee of security against a native population which could never be really trusted.   Men had only to look from their houses at its sombre ramparts to know that, come what may, they could never be overwhelmed.   Over two hundred yards long!   There had never been anything like it in the history of Bengal.

The 'ground floor' of the Fort—the vast flat surface with its fortifications and buildings—had not, in fact, been built at ground level.   In order to obtain the height necessary to fire down on any attackers, it had been constructed above enormous warehouses eighteen feet high, roofed in with a massive covering of stone strong enough to support every building the servants of the Company needed.   It was an extraordinary architectural achievement for those days, and it must have been rather like walking on the deck of a battleship, with the warehouses below connected by a honeycomb of damp, rat-infested passages.

More than half the Fort's 'deck' was taken up with an enormous parade-ground, bounded on the east by an arcade of heavy stone arches and on the west by the splendour of the Governor's residence, which was, incredibly, nearly two hundred and fifty feet long.   The northern boundary of the parade-ground consisted of a row of small buildings called Writers' Row which split the Fort into two sections. The Row was a series of damp, unhealthy, cell-like rooms which were used as lodgings by the young apprentices (called writers), and a small passage through Writers' Row linked the Fort's southern and northern sections.

If the southern half of the Fort, with its spacious parade-ground, its arcades, and a graceful colonnade leading from the Governor's House to the river, had the languid air of a residential section, the area north of Writers' Row was where the work was done. Here, crowded and bustling with activity (at least until lunch-time) was the heart of the Company's business. Offices for the writers, clerks and council members; the treasure-chamber guarded by a heavy old door with iron hinges; near by were the arms magazine and the military and food stores. A dispensary stood cheek by jowl with a laboratory; there was even a grog shop. All were grouped round the flagpole on which the British flag of the East India Company drooped listlessly. No wonder the Fort was looked upon as a symbol of might and security. And no wonder, too, that its secure walls served as an excuse for lethargy, incompetence and, worst of all, co mplacency.

The Governor of Calcutta at this crucial moment was a man of thirty-four. Roger Drake was accepted, if disliked, despite his many failings and inadequacies. He had been promoted to this position only four years ago for the simple reason that he happened to be the senior Company official. For that was the way the Company invariably managed its affairs, and who in the settlement was likely to quibble over Company rules while busily making a fortune?

It was a situation, however, with certain subtleties. Actually, Drake had only been appointed Acting-Governor, and as the years went by with no word from Leadenhall Street confirming his official position, the merchants of the settlement rightly presumed this was due to lack of confidence, so that William Tooke, a Company accountant, was not alone in saying that his invidious position made him 'appear very cheap among the natives'. (Ironically, Drake's title was confirmed in February 1756, but the letter did not reach Calcutta until after the siege.)

One has a picture of the man, not only incapable of inspiring the garrison throughout the siege, but, even worse, of never once having taken any steps to prevent the initial quarrel exploding into open warfare. He was pompous and vain, incapable of requesting or accepting advice. Since his authority had never been confirmed, he took every opportunity to assert it. He had a weak face, irresolute eyes, an accentuated paunch imprisoned in tight trousers, soft, uncertain hands that played nervously with each other—all middle-aged signposts to youth's deterioration. Already at the age of thirty-four his pomposity was a screen to hide his vanished ambitions. He was a man born to take second place, and Calcutta's tragedy was that he had been elevated to a position where it was more important for him to think than to act, to set an example rather than look to higher authority for a lead. His personal life was complicated, too; for after his first wife died he had married her sister—an act regarded as monstrous two hundred years ago. Calcutta never forgave him, and few of the English women spoke to Mrs Drake unless it became unavoidable. It was hardly surprising in these circumstances that the Governor grew embittered and started 'keeping indifferent company and'

—to quote Tooke again—'committing a thousand little meannesses'.

Had Drake been well served by his subordinates, had he been capable of taking advice, the coming disaster might have been averted. But it was not his custom to listen to the few intelligent members of the Council, and when they did speak, their words passed unheeded. The two senior members on whom Drake relied—Charles Manningham and William Frankland—were both inept and totally absorbed in financial speculation, yet because of the Governor's favouritism, they dominated the affairs of Calcutta and hid its deficiencies.

The commander of the garrison, Captain-Commandant George Minchin, was even more unfitted to meet a critical emergency. A thin, dark, saturnine man, his heavy beard a black splash against his scarlet tunic, Minchin was both indolent and stupid. Not once had he taken the trouble to study Calcutta's defences. Nor did he know until the last moment how many men he could count on, while the state of his guns hardly appeared to interest him. He did not know how much powder there was in the magazine, nor that most of it was damp. Yet to the very end—until he too deserted—he maintained a façade of efficiency, refusing all advice from his junior officers on whom the burden of the fighting was to fall.

As for the long-drawn-out quarrel that was to lead to war, its origins and the means by which some settlement could have been achieved without courting disaster will shortly become apparent. But it is important first to complete the picture of life in Calcutta at the time of the siege. The plans of the time give us excellent material, but these ancient charts are unfeeling; the roads along which the retreating garrison hauled their guns are so many brief, black lines; the big houses where trapped

men fought against ferocious odds are represented only
by dead, unfeeling squares. Since the battle for Calcutta
raged in almost every house, those who lived in them and
played a significant part must be introduced, for the
story of the siege is above all a story of human beings,
and the light that shines through it is of the unflinching
bravery of those who battled on, fighting not only a cruel
and merciless enemy, but treachery and cowardice among
the leaders whom they trusted.

During the weeks before the monsoon, a deadly cloak of
languor enveloped the city. No wind stirred, not even
down by the Hoogly river; the woodwork was hot to
the touch; the heat and sweat penetrated every corner
relentlessly, so that no man could escape their debilitating
effect. Children fretted, women complained as they
gasped, fanning themselves, in the big airless rooms of
the magnificent houses that ringed three sides of The
Park, the centre of Calcutta's social life, where every
breathless evening the Europeans took their stroll.

The Park was situated opposite the Fort and was
separated from it by a dusty road. It was a large, rect-
angular, tree-studded patch of green in a dusty waste,
each side more than a quarter of a mile long, and it had
been constructed out of a confusion of swamp and thick
palm and mangrove plantations previously shrouded in
an evil miasma from stinking drains. Now it was transformed, every trace of foliage save for a few ornamental
clumps of palms, flame- and tulip-trees hacked down to
encourage the slightest breeze. Oleander and hibiscus
lined the dusty walks that broke the carefully watered
grass round the flat, still water of the 'Great Tank', the
large man-made lake in its centre.

Along The Park's north side ran Calcutta's main

street, known as The Avenue. It began near the east gate of Fort William, and ran in a straight line to the left of The Park until it reached the north-east corner where a new playhouse had been built. Close by stood that hallmark of civilization—the new gaol. By the standards of the time The Avenue was a fine road, pot-holed no doubt, but wide enough for two carriages to pass in comfort, and on its left, as one walked up it from the Fort, stood St Anne's Church (which had lost its spire in a gale some years previously) among several magnificent houses.

Once it had passed the Playhouse, The Avenue gradually deteriorated, but if one turned right at the Playhouse along Rope Walk, the houses were, if anything, more imposing. For here, and south of The Park, the building boom had changed the face of Calcutta. Once the British residents had discovered a way to make local bricks—there was not a single stone on the swampy banks of the Hoogly—merchant after merchant had spent fortunes endeavouring to surpass the architectural efforts of his rivals, building Georgian houses over a hundred feet long, some with a dozen immense rooms, surrounded by compounds with cookhouses, bakeries, domestic quarters, stables and gardens for growing English vegetables. And if there were still no glass panes in the windows of these magnificent houses (they were too difficult to transport from England), at least a senior employee of the East India Company in 'White Town'—as this section of Calcutta was called—could boast twenty servants and half a dozen horses for his family.

Abruptly the calm magnificence of its houses changed at the turn of a street into the misery and squalor of 'Black Town', where, in the unyielding hostile sun the squatting sellers of fruit, flesh and fowl, of rice, herbs and *ghee*, clamoured each day for custom as the Europeans' servants did their shopping. Dust, flies, heat, sweat; rich, poor, the unfortunate, the oppressed; all made their way in a never-ending stream past mounds of rice spilling at their feet, hillocks of melons piled on the dusty brown ground, circular trays of sickly sweetmeats half hidden under their crusts of busy, moving flies.

From miles around the hopeful traders came in to relieve the misery of their everyday lives with a busy hour on the edge of this great city alive with movement, colour and life. The colour must have shrieked: the violence of a basket of oranges, a paler heap of lemons, made a man thirsty. So did pineapples, green and brown and tufted; sliced water-melons, pink and spotted black, the spots like the flies that crowded the market, never defeated, crawling over everything.

This was the other part of the picture; but for the Europeans life was good in Calcutta—which, by the summer of 1756, had grown to such a size that the mansions of White Town sprawled more than a mile along the bank of the Hoogly and a quarter of a mile inland, while the jumbled confusion of mud and reed huts, fragile but swarming like an antheap with the life and movement of two hundred thousand natives, extended the city's boundaries to almost three miles.

All this had happened in less than seventy years; since the day Job Charnock arrived on the mud-flats of the Hoogly begging for the right to live in a thatched hut and trade. By 1756 the East India Company, by strategy, by avarice (and doubtless by good luck), all but embraced a continent.

The Company made its own laws, mustered its own armies, marshalled its own police, and though it lived and traded only by the sufferance of India's great potentates, its bounty was so great, its presence so profitable, that in all but name it ruled vast foreign dominions never seen by the masters of Leadenhall Street. With the growth of the Company, however, there had also grown a danger perhaps not apparent to those in London: that arrogance was prevailing at the price of prudence.

Every evening the owners and their families promenaded in The Park, emerging from their houses which fronted it on three sides (the Fort forming the fourth) in their most elaborate finery, regardless of the climate. Heavy broadcloth coats hung over vivid brocaded waistcoats. Frilly cuffs of silk shirts dangled over the wrists. Thick breeches, fastened with knee-bands, imprisoned the heat at one end, tight neckbands at the other. Swords were a necessary encumbrance. Wigs and three-cornered hats prickled the scalp.

It must have been a handsome sight. Ornate palanquins drawing up along The Avenue, their bearers gently setting down their human cargoes; the Governor's carriage rumbling by; the ladies in the vivid fashions of only a year earlier; the children playing, or stopping to watch the Indians performing their tricks. Here was the snake-charmer tapping his basket, taking up his bamboo reed, the cobra obligingly rearing up in a sensuous curve and hissing; the sword-swallower thrusting the sword into his mouth and holding out a skinny, scarred hand for a few annas; the juggler throwing four brass balls round his head with such speed one could hardly see them separately as they formed a continuous circle.

One had merely to walk round The Park to see the splendid mansions of almost every man and woman who was to become involved in the siege. Gervas Bellamy, the senior chaplain, had lived on The Avenue for thirty years, close to his church. He was a corpulent man, whose heavy frame consumed much energy in the unceasing heat. Layers of fat from good living had given his jowls a rubbery, bulldog look, yet his face was happy and he hardly looked like a preacher. But then, he was no ordinary parson. By the age of sixty-five he had made a fortune, quite legally, by trading privately during the years he preached publicly. He was reputed to have the best claret and madeira in Calcutta, which he drank in some quantity.

Bellamy was to play an important role in the drama of the siege, as was his youngest daughter Anna, an unspoiled girl of sixteen, tall and fair, already ripening in the subtle way women mature early in the tropics. Two sons were to be equally involved: John, the younger, a cheerful, carefree lieutenant of twenty-one, and Thomas, his exact opposite, a morose man of twenty-six.

Within a stone's throw of Bellamy's home lived his assistant chaplain Robert Mapletoft, a man of thirty-two, with his wife Sarah, who was expecting their third child at any moment. No chaplain ever chose his own assistant in the East India Company, and one can be sure that Bellamy would never have chosen Mapletoft. A tall, thin man in his clerical black, the skin close to his bones, he not only looked weak, he obviously hated Calcutta—or was it, perhaps, that his bitter, complaining wife hated it and, as so often happens, had transmitted her loathing to her husband?

Just behind The Avenue, on the fringe of the two 'towns', Mary Carey, the sixteen-year-old half-caste wife of a British sailor, lived modestly and respectably with her Indian mother, waiting for Peter to return from each voyage, little suspecting she was destined to be the only woman to live through the night in the Black Hole.

Her small house was hidden behind the most ostentatious building on The Avenue, within cannon shot of the Fort, owned by Omichand, a Jain merchant and the richest man in the settlement. He alone of the Hindus lived in White Town—a privilege that could hardly be denied him since he had financed the building of the majority of the European houses.

In forty years of trading, Omichand had amassed half a million pounds, and as well as his mansion in White Town he owned a large private garden and a house on the outskirts of Calcutta. Almost every person in Calcutta had at one time or another been enmeshed in his business dealings. He lent money to those who had lost heavily at whist or at five-card loo. He financed the trading in which the Company permitted its employees to engage; for how could a young writer fresh out of England possibly find the necessary capital? Omichand provided it with a smile, and since most of the articles yielded a hundred per cent profit, he was content with half. Omichand, too, had long played a special role as intermediary between the Nabob and the British, although recently the latter had tended to place less reliance on him since they had uncovered increasing evidence of his unscrupulous dealings.

He was now so obese that his carriage had had to be built specially for him, with low steps and firmer, stronger handles; out of it he could be seen struggling and grunting, while two guards stood by with drawn scimitars. He bulged in all directions from the silk gown which reached to his feet. Priceless rings were imprisoned in the creases of his fat fingers, and as he held out a hand in greeting, the whole mountain of flesh quivered.

The very flesh of this man who was to help in the betrayal of Calcutta indicated greed. It shone out of two tiny darting black eyes sunk like fragments of coal in rolls of fat; eyes that were never still; not cruel eyes but cold and appraising.

The east side of The Park—where The Avenue turned sharp right—was bounded by Rope Walk, and the most imposing house along this dusty thoroughfare belonged to Lady Russell, a remarkable widow who lived alone. Short in stature, with an equally short temper, she had buried two husbands. Many people disliked her, perhaps not realizing that her rudeness was a shield thrown up by her loneliness. Russell had been her first husband, and after his death she remarried, but when her second husband died, she reverted to her first husband's name and title.

There were not many houses on Rope Walk, for this newly constructed roadway was too distant from the river, and Lady Russell had few neighbours apart from William Dumbleton, Calcutta's notary, who lived a hundred yards away with his wife and two children.

South of The Park stood many of the largest houses crowded close together. Minchin lived here in a mansion that was to be the scene of the most heroic stand of the siege. Grant, the adjutant, was near by; so were Manningham and Frankland. Not far away was Lieutenant Witherington, in whose incompetent hands lay the garrison's powder-train. And lastly, near the Hoogly, almost the last house in White Town belonged to John Zephaniah Holwell, the Zemindar or chief magistrate, by far the shrewdest man in Calcutta.

Holwell took his walk in The Park with the same vigorous determination that characterized all his actions and which had made him, in the six years since he took office, one of the most respected (if slightly feared) men in the settlement. For in six years Holwell had increased the Company's revenue and rents by £10,000 a year; not by imposing new or increasing old taxes, but by reforming abuses and frauds. Originally he had been trained as a surgeon at Guy's, and had later become a lawyer. He was forty-five, not tall, although he gave that impression, and powerfully-built. Above his cheeks a criss-cross of tiny wrinkles fanned out from the corners of his eyes, and though he could smile readily, the contours etched by the sun on his solid face always made him look stern.

Holwell took a brisk walk almost every evening. So did the younger men—the sons of merchants, the writers, and junior officers. A writer started young. Henry Lushington, for instance, had been apprenticed to the East India Company at the age of fifteen, and already, three years later, was invaluable as a translator of the Company's documents through his knowledge of Persian and Indian dialects. Though his salary was only £5 a year, he had the normal rights to trade privately and had already negotiated (with Omichand's help) two profitable cargoes of raw silk to Britain. Like other boys of his age, he had to work hard; but the hours were short and when work was over there was boating on the Hoogly, fishing for mango fish or shooting for snipe or teal.

On some evenings there would be dancing at the Playhouse (though there was a great shortage of young ladies), or amateur dramatics, or sing-songs to the fiddling of Janniko, a half-caste Portuguese—one of the score of men who had no direct service with the Company but who had somehow settled there, so that by 1756 Calcutta boasted half a dozen private tailors, four butchers, carpenters, farriers, coachmen and, most important, six fiddlers.

The young men were well-behaved—they had to be or they would have been thrown out—which was certainly something that could not be said for the half-caste soldiers who formed the majority of the garrison.

Arrack, the local drink, was cheap. Licensed prostitutes (another source of revenue to the Company) were available in the sordid, smelly alleys of Black Town. Sailors from visiting Indiamen were constantly involved in fights with the Dutch mercenaries, so that the respectable peace and quiet of Calcutta was regularly shattered as drunken soldiers were thrown into the Black Hole for a night.

The Black Hole had no connection with the settlement's civilian gaol. It was a military prison that had been built almost by accident. Some years previously a double row of arches had been constructed along the east wall of the Fort so that they looked across the parade-ground to the Governor's residence. The fifteen arches in each row rested on heavy circular columns of solid masonry, forming an arcade in which soldiers could walk protected from the sun or blinding monsoon rains. Behind them was the actual wall of the east curtain, and at some time the arches had been divided by cross-walling, forming separate partitions in which soldiers could wait for their spell of duty or parades. Though these partitions were of course open to the parade-ground, the roof of the arcade was so low that the partitions were stiflingly hot beneath their vaulted ceilings.

The last two arches—the fourteenth and fifteenth—had been completely walled in to form one room with two small barred air-holes and a door. This was the prison: a room about eighteen feet by fourteen feet, intended to house at the most three or four drunken soldiers for a night. Its dim interior was as hot as an oven, only pencils of light coming through the windows which looked out into the arcade, made dark by the low arches.

The room was filled with the stench of sweat, foul air, urine, excrement and rats. Along the wall at the rear ran a platform on which soldiers could sleep. It was the only furniture except for a pot.

The quarrel whose disastrous repercussions were to bear the undistinguished nickname of this sordid little hole had never before been so menacing. True, the merchants were familiar with frequent outbursts of wounded Moslem pride but invariably they had been resolved without violence. A handsome gift or a cash present (the British were always being blackmailed) worked wonders; soothing words and elaborate courtesies to the reigning nabob cost nothing but swallowed pride, yet had proved equally efficacious. And then, suddenly, everything seemed to change and almost without realizing what had happened or how it happened, the British in Calcutta found themselves innocent pawns in a bitter, personal vendetta between Drake and the Moslem ruler; therefore one must trace—however briefly—the causes of the dispute.

The Kingdom of Bengal was a province, in theory subject to the Emperors of Delhi, which, with the passing of years had become governed by all-powerful Moslem nabobs, whose seat was Murshidabad, one hundred and sixty miles from Calcutta. By race and religion they were foreign to the Hindu population, but as trade with the British increased, the nabobs' share of the profits grew so great that their power increased correspondingly and they maintained an iron Moslem grip over the Hindus. Yet it was the Hindus—men such as Omichand—who ran the commerce of the country, and many saw in the powerful European settlements the only possible allies who might one day help them to overthrow the Moslem dynasty which had oppressed them for five centuries. Not unnaturally, the Moslems realized the dangers of the close associations between the Europeans and the

Hindus, thrown together in the common interest of trade, and when the Europeans began to erect fortifications (mainly against dacoits) their obvious reaction was one of immediate alarm.   Since the trade of the British exceeded that of all the other foreign traders, including the French and the Dutch, they became the prime target for suspicion.

This is an over-simplification, but without question the Moslem distrust of the British stemmed from this problem.   It was, however, kept within bounds.   There had been no question of war; and indeed, relations between the nabobs and the British, though broken by sporadic outbursts of Moslem rage, had been fairly good on the whole.

Aliverdi Khan (the predecessor of Siraj-Uddaula who was to march on Calcutta) summed up his attitude to the British succinctly by comparing them to a hive of bees, 'of whose honey you might reap benefit, but if you disturbed their hive they would sting you to death'.   It was never in his mind to drive out the European settlements of hard-working merchants who brought so much gold to his treasury, and indeed, during the early years of his reign he had allowed the British to build the Maratha Ditch, a moat planned to surround Calcutta which had never been finished.   There had been a good reason for Aliverdi's tolerance.   For ten years he had been engaged in a long struggle with the warlike Marathas, and since he was not averse to British trade. he realized they must be allowed to protect their settlements.

Siraj-Uddaula was from a very different mould.   He was only twenty-seven when the old man died in April 1756 at the age of eighty-two, but long before he had started plotting to secure the throne.   His vices have probably been exaggerated with the years, but he was certainly cruel to such an extent that one of his own relatives, the Moslem historian Ghulam Husain Khan, was to write that he indulged in every caprice; 'making no distinction between vice and virtue, and paying no regard to the nearest relations, he carried defilement wherever he went, and, like a man alienated in his mind, he made the houses of men and women of distinction the scenes of his profligacy, without minding either rank or station. In a little time he became as detested as Pharaoh, and people on meeting him by chance used to say, "God save us from him." '

Siraj-Uddaula, suspicious of all foreigners, hated the British, but most of all he hated Governor Drake, and during the last fatal illness of Aliverdi Khan, when power was virtually in his hands, the series of disputes was changing in a dangerous way from a mere difference of opinion between Court and Council to a bitter personal animosity between Siraj-Uddaula and Roger Drake.

The British were partly to blame. As the old man lay dying of dropsy, merchants such as Manningham and Frankland were extending their custom-free rights to certain Hindu favourites, who thus escaped dues which should have gone to the Nabob. They levied duties they had no right to impose, taxed marriages and the transfer of property, causing 'eternal clamour and complaints . . . at Court'.

Siraj-Uddaula, impatiently waiting to become Nabob and the ruler of Bengal, was well aware of this state of affairs. His spies were everywhere. The British, he said, were robbing him (and he was right). They were secretly building fortifications (and he was wrong). And above all, the personal and fatal animosity was growing between the Nabob and the Governor in Calcutta as the incidents increased.

At the beginning of March, little more than a month before Aliverdi died, the British were to make a fatal blunder. As the old Nabob lay on his sick-bed, Siraj-Uddaula was busily engaged in ensuring his own succession. The majority of his rivals had died (or been murdered), but there remained his aunt—the eldest daughter of Aliverdi—and her son, Kissendass. Siraj-Uddaula was not slow to deal with his aunt, but Kissendass—the potential rival—departed with his wife and a large fortune to take refuge in Calcutta.

The British were certainly not entirely to blame for allowing such a dangerous situation to develop. Kissendass, a man of some wiliness, innocently announced that he was making a pilgrimage to Orissa. Unknown to anyone at Court, he then indirectly approached William Watts, the chief of the East India Company's small station at Cossimbazar, only twelve miles from the capital city of Murshidabad, requesting permission to rest awhile in Calcutta as his wife was expecting a child.

Watts unaccountably never troubled to discuss the matter with his council at Cossimbazar, but merely wrote a letter to Drake recommending that Kissendass be allowed to stay in Calcutta until his wife's baby was born. To give asylum, even temporary, to any contender for power was incredibly foolish, and the only charitable explanation for Watts's action is that his wife was also expecting a baby and he was moved by sympathy.

Kissendass arrived in Calcutta on March 13. Drake was away, visiting a near-by settlement, but Watts's letter of recommendation was accepted in his absence by Manningham. And Kissendass immediately moved his family—and a great deal of treasure—into Omichand's house on The Avenue.

Within forty-eight hours Siraj-Uddaula was fully aware of what had happened. (It is remarkable that messengers were able to move through the trackless miles between Calcutta and Murshidabad in such a short time.) Understandably, the heir apparent flew into a rage, and although unable to take any positive action while Aliverdi still lived, he ordered the chief of his own intelligence service to dispatch spies to Calcutta and report every aspect of British activity. His next action was to make his anger plain to Watts, who became seriously alarmed and sent Drake an urgent message suggesting that Kissendass be expelled from Calcutta in the shortest possible time.

Drake flatly refused, although Holwell begged him to accept Watts's advice. Even Bellamy, who had lived longer in Calcutta than any other Englishman, called on the Governor to expostulate. But Drake obstinately refused to budge; so Kissendass stayed. Siraj-Uddaula immediately believed that Drake was either plotting to help his rival, or had been bribed. In fact, neither supposition was true. Drake was merely a fool, constitutionally incapable of listening to well-informed advice.

Had Drake been wise enough to have second thoughts, had he even had sufficient sense to listen to the counsel of men like Holwell, Grant and Bellamy, history might have been written very differently. But at this critical juncture, when considered statesmanship was vital, the Council in Calcutta was in a state of friction. Manningham and Frankland were sowing discord. Relations among the others were so strained that Minchin never spoke to the Governor, and since Drake had great faith in Minchin's second-in-command, Captain Clayton, Minchin hardly spoke to him either. So tense was the atmosphere that Holwell was virtually ostracized for offering suggestions which had no direct relation to his particular duties. Minchin snubbed him publicly. And, exacerbating the whole ridiculous situation, was the determination of Drake, Manningham and Frankland that when the troubled times through which they were living had somehow resolved themselves, the army must in no circumstances receive any credit in Leadenhall Street.

The first question that strikes one today is why nobody seemed to take any positive action to arrest the mounting tension, but as the story unfolds—a story set, remember, in a humid, enervating heat—it becomes more understandable.

There were several factors. Men such as Bellamy knew, of course, that Siraj-Uddaula had hated the British long before he gained the throne. He knew what the presence of Kissendass in Calcutta implied. But for thirty years Bellamy had lived through recurring troubles with the Indians, and it had never come to a fight. One can imagine him saying that though the Moors were always threatening, they took good care never to attack Fort William. And indeed, one senses, reading the old papers, a complacency similar to that which smothered England just prior to World War II. So many threats had been made over the years that they had long since become a sort of devalued vocal currency, worth no more than Hitler's empty threats.

Most men in Calcutta were middle-class merchants whose interest lay wholly in making as much money as they could as rapidly as possible, and before the siege, before the appearance of a different stamp of soldier and administrator such as Clive and Hastings, few of the inhabitants had much pretension to intelligence. They were plodders, not geniuses; they had the mediocre attributes required by the East India Company, which shunned any men who might cause trouble with the Indians when all the Company wanted was a quiet life and regular profits.

A man such as Holwell might be far-seeing enough

to realize the full gravity of the situation, but there was still nothing he could do. The protocol of the hierarchy in Calcutta was rigid. The Governor's power was absolute. There was no question of writing to London— and even if a man had done so, he would have received no thanks from Leadenhall Street. As trade had prospered, as the ramifications of the East India Company had expanded, it had become too powerful to be aware of all that was going on, and too arrogant to thank its employees for emphasizing the fact. Yet the war that was to result in the fall of Calcutta—and, ironically, in the birth of the British Empire—might still have been averted. The two antagonists were growling at each other, but no more.

Then a new incident set them on. The British and French were already fighting in Europe (though war had not been officially declared), and warnings from Europe arrived at both the British and French settlements in Bengal. British and French now started to repair their fortifications, although only on a trifling scale. The French, however, spread rumours (and saw to it that Siraj-Uddaula heard them) that the British were making preparations for the arrival of a large force. Nothing could have been further from the truth, but Siraj-Uddaula invariably distrusted the English and within ten days of Aliverdi's death on April 10, he sent a sharp demand to both British and French settlements to pull down all fortifications erected since the start of Aliverdi's illness.

The French treated the Nabob's emissary courteously and sent the new Nabob a message telling him that they had built no new fortifications but had only repaired one bastion damaged by lightning, an explanation Siraj-Uddaula accepted.

Not so the British. Drake wrote an incredibly foolish

letter in which he said: '. . . that in the late War between our Nation and the French, they had attacked and taken the Town of Madras Contrary to the neutrality We expected would have been preserved in the Mogull's Dominions; and that there being present great appearance of another War between the Two Crowns, We were under some apprehension they would act in the same way in Bengal, to prevent which We were only repairing our Line of Guns to the Water-side.'

The effect was electric. On receiving the letter, the Nabob jumped from his seat and, drawing his sword, cried, 'Who shall dare to think of commencing hostilities in my country, or presume to imagine that I have not the power to protect them?'

It must have been on this day that he finally decided to attack the British. Drake's letter was only the final spark that ignited the explosion. For years now he had distrusted their promises not to interfere with the government of Bengal. They had abused their trading rights. He knew the Hindus hated the Moslem rulers. The British still harboured Kissendass, his rival to the throne.

The ordinary men and women in Calcutta knew little or nothing of these grave events, though some news must have filtered through. Holwell must certainly have discussed his experiences at council meetings with friends like Bellamy. But however disturbing the rumours, the inhabitants were content to leave the outcome in the hands of soldiers whose only duty in Calcutta was expressly to attend to their protection, or doubtless they relied on the diplomacy of the Governor and his aides. Foolish they may have been, but in a community cooped up in an alien land—from which it took up to twelve months for a letter to reach England—the heat, the dust, the flies, could be borne more easily than the knowledge that they had virtually no contact with the outside world, and this sense of isolation magnified the importance (and the abilities) of those in command.

There was little time left. On the evening of May 28, the Nabob sent for his letterwriter, who crouched at his feet as Siraj-Uddaula composed a letter that would be read and re-read by historians long after those who fought the battle of Calcutta were dead.

For some unexplained reason it was addressed to Coja Wajid, an Armenian merchant who often acted as intermediary. No doubt the Nabob told Coja Wajid to make certain Drake read it.

'It has been my design', the Nabob dictated, 'to level the English fortifications raised within my jurisdiction on account of their great strength. As I have nothing at present to divert me from the execution of that resolution, I am determined to make use of this opportunity. For which reason I shall use the utmost expedition in my march that I may arrive before Calcutta as soon as possible. Should any person plead ever so strongly on their behalf, it will avail them nothing.'

The Nabob read the words carefully, then suddenly snatching the pen from the startled letter-writer, scrawled across the bottom of the page, 'I swear by the great God and the prophets that unless the English consent to fill up their Ditch, raze their fortifications, I will totally expel them from the country.'

On June 5 the Nabob's army surrounded the British factory at Cossimbazar. On its surrender, Watts, the Governor, was thrown into a common prison.

It was an omen of worse to come.

CHAPTER TWO

The Last Days of Peace

Tuesday, June 15—Thursday, 17

The reaction in Calcutta to the news of the fall of Cossimbazar set a pattern that was to become lamentably
familiar: stunned disbelief, confusion, wrangling and a
total and frightening incapacity to form any intelligent
plan for the defence of the city and its Fort.

Drake was with Manningham when the fatal packet
of thick parchment reached him. It had been carried
the one hundred and fifty miles by a *kasid*, an Indian
postal messenger, in the remarkable time of twenty-
seven hours. Tearing it open, he read the news silently
before handing it to Manningham, and then, white with
a fury he could not control, he seized the letter back,
re-read it, crumpled it up and hurled it on the floor. One
can understand his consternation—yet, was the news so
unexpected?

It should not have been, for there had been ominous
warnings since the morning when Watts in Cossimbazar had awakened to find his fort surrounded by the
Nabob's troops. The neighbouring forts of the French
and the Dutch were also encircled and Watts probably
assumed this show of force was merely the prelude to
some new attempt at extortion. Such demonstrations
were not infrequent and often lasted over several days,
successive nabobs having discovered that the longer their

troops sat firmly outside the forts, the higher the price the foreigners would pay to see them go. Watts, therefore, probably totally misinterpreting the presence of the soldiers, sent a message to Drake urging him to write submissive letters to the Nabob.

Drake, back in Calcutta, complied, but the messenger carrying his letters never arrived in Cossimbazar. Then, three days later, something happened which was totally unusual. Upsetting the normal, familiar routine of extortionist tactics, the Nabob's troops suddenly withdrew from the French and Dutch posts, leaving Watts in the British fort still menacingly invested. Thoroughly alarmed, he got another message through to Drake asking for reinforcements.

Although Watts's force numbered only fifty men, the Council in Calcutta—for reasons never clearly understood—refused to send help. Watts was now in a difficult position. Cossimbazar was obviously in serious danger. It ought to be held. After all, it was the gateway to the vital settlement at Calcutta. Yet all Watts's twenty years' experience in Bengal warned him against making a fight for the fort. Were he—as the servant of a trading company—to do so, he could expect no thanks unless success accompanied such a drastic step. And there was no chance of success. Besides, the Nabob's troops did not appear very truculent—indeed, they even permitted him to send out for supplies—and though the fact that only the British fort was surrounded was ominous, the formula in other respects was normal enough to suggest that this dispute, like so many others, might eventually be solved by some financial settlement. Consequently, when he was told the Nabob wished to receive him, he saw no reason to refuse the invitation, and set off accompanied by the doctor who served as surgeon in the fort.

However, hardly were they clear of the walls when they were seized by soldiers. Watts's arms were pinioned tightly behind his back and, speechless with mortification, he was taken before the Nabob, who looked at him coldly for a few moments, then curtly told an officer to detain Watts and the doctor as prisoners.

Faced with this shock, the garrison of the tiny fort was powerless. Within a few hours the fort capitulated. There was no fighting. Mrs Watts was allowed to move to the French fort. Lieutenant Elliot fired the only shot of the engagement, killing himself rather than suffer the shame of surrender.

It was June 5, and the same day, in the hottest season of the year, the Nabob started his historic march south, taking Watts with him, his artillery swollen by nearly eighty cannon which he had seized.

The advance must have been vastly impressive. One French report recounts that it took half a day for the Nabob's army to pass their fort on its way south, and since no effort at concealment was required, it marched to the martial, if dissonant, music of three bands; each consisted of thirty big drums and a hundred kettledrums, beating irregular time. Their cacophony had no rhythm, for each drummer played as an individual. Heading the force came the eighteen thousand cavalry which were the Nabob's special pride. A fearless horseman himself (who always kept a thousand mounts ready for battle in Murshidabad), he led the cavalry divisions, sometimes on horseback, at other times carried by four men in his palanquin, ornately painted and studded with silver nails.

The artillery followed under the command of a French renegade, the Marquis de St Jacques, who had been expelled from the French fort of Chandernagore following a quarrel over a woman. St Jacques had now been in the service of the Nabob for some time and had recruited several other French gunners with promises of high pay and indifferent opposition in battle. Among them was Jean-Baptiste Gentil, who had also fled from Chandernagore. Originally an infantryman, he was apparently invaluable in handling the hundreds of complex transport problems involved in hauling the guns over the trackless route. Each cannon was so heavy that it had to be pulled by up to thirty yoke of oxen, while four hundred war-trained elephants lumbered behind, ready to push them over difficult ground. Each animal in the column was decked with flags or pennants, even down to the two thousand camels which belched and grunted beneath the loads of stores and followed in the wake of thirty thousand ragged foot-soldiers, some armed with muskets, others with a variety of implements ranging from spears or sabres to bows and arrows.

The terrain was so rough and difficult that no attempt was made to keep the ranks serried. At times the army marched abreast in a series of great squares; at others, it straggled in near confusion, stretching out for miles. And at the rear came a sinister addition to the army: some seven thousand professional plunderers who stripped each village lying in its path.

One can readily understand the awe with which the villagers regarded this vast body of men. What is harder to understand is the complete lack of any sense of urgency in Calcutta, soon less than a hundred miles distant in the army's line of march. Surely the threat must have been starkly clear? Every report coming in of the size and strength of the Nabob's forces, of the speed at which they marched, indicated only one thing—a full-scale siege. One would have expected the contemporary reports (and excuses) to indicate feverish preparations and desperate measures.

What was happening? Why was food not requisitioned? Nor trenches dug? Where were the reports on the powder stocks? What provision could the small hospital make for the wounded? What would happen to the women and children? These and a hundred other elementary questions apparently received no attention, perhaps because, as Captain Grant, the adjutant, said, 'such was the levity of the times that severe measures were not esteemed necessary'. Instead, the Council appears to have spent hours wrangling among themselves or composing letters appealing to Madras for reinforcements.

From this distance of time (which does give us a certain advantage) it now seems so obvious. If the Nabob were really going to attack Calcutta, then every hour of preparation and planning counted. If, on the other hand, his march southwards was merely a bluff, then it was vital the Fort organized a show of force sufficiently impressive to put the Council in a strong position where they could negotiate in order to achieve a settlement.

It is recorded that Drake did hold a council of war to discuss what measures should be taken, but its members seem to have spent the entire morning listening to recitals of the state of the defences of the Fort itself. These now appeared melancholy beyond belief. The walls of the east curtain facing The Park had been broken in several places to let light and air into the warehouses—and had never been repaired. A large warehouse had been erected against the south wall in such a manner that it prevented any flanking fire from either of the two south bastions. The roof of this warehouse, it was suddenly discovered, was not strong enough to bear cannon. The walls of the Fort were crumbling in many places, the woodwork was often so rotten it could not support a gun-carriage. During the lush, fat

years of profit-making, not a soul appears to have had
the energy to examine the Fort or set the idle garrison
to work repairing its defences and deficiencies.

Leach, the Company carpenter and a loyal servant of
long standing, conducted the gloomy Council round the
walls. The neglect was all too plain and at scores of
places the guns could no longer be mounted. Leading
them along the eastern parapet, he tore off a chunk of
decaying wood. Every beam was rotten; no cannon had
been mounted there for years. The carriages themselves
were so eaten away that twenty-six had to be condemned
out of hand. On the banks of the Hoogly, near the
Governor's wharf, fifty cannon—eighteen- and twenty-
four-pounders—which had arrived in Calcutta three
years previously were found rusted and useless with their
cannon-balls; all had been left there since the day they
were unloaded and dumped on the river bank.

Not until the following day did Drake remember to
ask for the first time about the Fort's reserves of powder.
During a Council meeting, Lieutenant Witherington, in
charge of the ammunition train, was sent for, and to the
Governor's relief calmly told him that never in all
Calcutta's history had there been such ample stocks of
powder. His first report, however, omitted the news
that almost all of it was damp.

When this became known, the Council, it appears,
was thrown into confusion and consternation. Nobody
had thought to store it in a dry place during the previous
monsoon. Hardly had this news confounded the Governor when it was found that the small quantity of grape-
shot had been lying so long it was worm-eaten. No shells
fitted the guns. No fuses had been prepared.

Endeavouring to choke down his personal hatred of
Minchin, the Governor was compelled to request a full
report on the strength of the garrison. Incredibly, Cap-

tain Minchin did not know. Clayton, his second-in-command, was sent for—and he did not know either. At last, with the help of Surgeon Gray of the hospital and Captain Grant, it was discovered that seventy European soldiers were in hospital. Nobody had the faintest idea of this until Gray was asked; twenty-five more had been sent to small stations up-country, almost all without the knowledge of senior officers. The total strength of the available garrison was in fact one hundred and eighty men—of which only forty-five were Europeans.

Even Drake's complacency was shattered by this news. He apparently worked himself into a fury and, telling Minchin that his conduct was outrageous, requested the captains of all vessels in the Hoogly to see how many volunteers they could spare. Plans were immediately started to form a militia, in which Holwell was appointed a captain.

At last Drake seems to have realized the one vital omission—there was no plan to defend the city. Consequently—and it now seems incredibly leisurely—another war council was held the following day, and we have a picture of that vital meeting when the only intelligent piece of advice (which might possibly have saved the Fort) was brutally disregarded.

The council chamber, situated in the Governor's residence, was a lofty room running the breadth of the building, so that while one set of glassless windows gave out on to the parade-ground (with the Black Hole across the other side), the other looked over the top of the colonnade leading to the Hoogly, where the ships were plainly visible lying at anchor. At the end of a long table, Drake sat in his chair which rested on a small dais he had had erected when he assumed office, as though to buttress his authority against his unpopularity. Along the length of the table were grouped the Council members, strengthened at this late moment by several non-members whose expert advice was now in urgent demand. The dress for council meetings was usually formal, the men wearing their finest broadcloth coats with silver facings, despite the heat. But many members took advantage of the crisis to attend in the light muslin Indian-style clothes which they wore in their crowded, stifling ffices, and some even wore small skull caps instead of wigs.

Drake had asked John O'Hara, the Company's chief engineer, to attend. O'Hara was only twenty-four, quick-tempered, and after two years in Calcutta frustrated to such a point that he could hardly hold his temper in face of the stupidity he saw around him.

The question which the Council was now discussing centred not so much on the defence of the Fort as on the larger problem of the defence of Calcutta. Obviously the whole city could not be held. What preoccupied their thoughts was their hold on their own splendid White Town.

O'Hara had nursed many grievances during his two years in the city. His attempts to repair the east wall of the Fort or the Maratha Ditch had continually been frustrated, usually because there was insufficient money to pay the coolies. Nobody would ever take the responsibility for expending money. They would write to London, they promised him, knowing that it would take two years to get a reply. But he happened to be very intelligent as well as extremely forthright, and he must have enjoyed himself more than at any other time in his life when Drake asked him to suggest a possible line of defence in White Town.

The engineer stood up, waited a full half-minute before replying, then staggered the Council by announcing bluntly that it would be impossible to defend White Town at all. In his opinion, the only chance of victory lay in blowing up or demolishing all the great houses surrounding the Fort, then fighting from the Fort itself.

The council members were startled to their feet in an uproar. Blow up their magnificent houses! The man must be mad! One officer was heard to growl that if you asked civilians military questions, you deserved to get stupid answers. Understandably, it was some time before order could be restored. When O'Hara was finally allowed to explain the reasons for his extraordinary proposition, he did so briefly. First, the garrison was not large enough to defend a long perimeter. Second, and more important, every building close to the Fort overtopped it by many feet, so that once the enemy were in occupation it would be a simple matter to fire down on the garrison's defenders. Third, the houses and roads which divided them would give the Indians magnificent cover when they attacked the Fort. They would be able to bring up their cannon under cover. O'Hara put his case well. If the houses were destroyed, he pointed out, the defenders in the Fort would be able to pour down fire from their protected positions on Indians who would have to advance over open ground.

His advice was sound. Over the years Calcutta's sky-line had risen piecemeal until its houses dwarfed the Fort, whose old walls were only eighteen feet high. Most of the houses which now overlooked it had large first-floor apartments topped with flat roofs, sometimes a hundred feet long and twice the height of the Fort.

O'Hara must have argued with some force for both Grant and Holwell supported him. But as Grant said later, 'so little credit was then given . . . that the Nabob would venture to attack us, or offer to force our lines' that any proposal to demolish the houses 'would have been thought ridiculous'.

Here was the core of the now inevitable tragedy. Right up until the very last minutes, Drake, Minchin, Manningham, Frankland and many of the others could hardly bring themselves to believe the Nabob would actually dare to attack. Still secure in their own houses, their private property, the tangible rewards of years of work in Bengal, they clung obstinately to the hope that the dispute could be resolved peacefully. Perhaps they might have been swayed had they been assured of some prospect of compensation, but what hope was there of this with England and a parsimonious Company so far away? Destroy their property? Only as a last desperate step—or so they felt. Yet had O'Hara's advice been taken, the outcome of the siege might have been totally different.

Holwell suggested a compromise. Why not destroy houses and walls near the perimeter of White Town, leaving three or four close to the Fort to be used as outposts? This suggestion was also brusquely vetoed, and the Council eventually decided on a plan more in harmony with their personal interests.

It was decided to draw a defence line through the houses in White Town, with batteries at the three main entrances. O'Hara was ordered to erect the batteries as soon as possible, palisade the smaller streets, demolish all bridges, and employ native coolies to dig a ditch across The Park.

The Council was about to break up when an Indian came in to Drake with a message. It was brief. The Nabob had issued an order forbidding all merchants or shopkeepers to supply the British with provisions.

Drake strode out white-faced, but at least the message had brought him to a sense of reality. That night he ordered the inhabitants to send all their arms and provisions into the Fort. Every able-bodied man was summoned 'by beat of drum' and the next morning the militia paraded: two hundred and fifty strong, including one hundred Europeans—many of whom, like Peter Carey, had been drawn from the crews of the ships in the Hoogly on the understanding that they were to be recalled if their captains wished. The rest were a strange and exotic mixture of half-castes and Armenians with no pretence or inclination to the military arts. A much more promising reinforcement appeared, however, as many young writers volunteered for temporary military duty.

For the first time it was now possible to establish the number of men under arms—military and militia. The count revealed a total of one hundred and eighty soldiers, including forty-five Europeans; fifty European volunteers; sixty European militia; one hundred and fifty Armenian and Portuguese militia; thirty-five European artillerymen; forty volunteers from the ships. In all, five hundred and fifteen men.

It was at this moment that Drake took an incomprehensible step. He appointed Manningham a Colonel and Frankland a Lieutenant-Colonel. The two men were, of course, well disposed to him and wielded much power behind the scenes. Drake's hatred of Captain Minchin was well known, but even so it was incredible that at this crucial moment he should promote two civilians over his garrison commander's head. Minchin was furious at this insult to his profession, and the immediate reaction among the officers loyal to him (or, to put it another way, his cronies) was a not unnatural feeling that war was hardly worth the candle if the glory went to the civilians.

It is not until now, on the Thursday or Friday (June 11 or 12) just four or five days before the siege, that one begins to sense a change of pace, a mood of urgency unaccountably missing beforehand. All the various reports and testimonies written later by the survivors bear this out. Every man tells his story with his own emphasis and these accounts are there to read. Oddly, they seem much occupied with the theoretical problems involved, but do not at first dwell on the early days of preparation. Then, suddenly, they all show a new alertness. It is curious, reading them; it is almost as though everyone in Calcutta had had the same bad dream and awakened on that one particular morning to find the dream reality.

Perhaps the one thing that stirred the people, many of them still unable to believe that the worst could happen, was the exodus of the Indians. At first only a few had left the settlement, but their numbers had grown, and by June 11 they were pouring out in a continuous stream until it was estimated some eighty thousand had fled into the surrounding countryside.

For the British, and more particularly for their wives, this was the biggest disaster ever experienced. Women who had never done a stroke of work since they settled in Calcutta now found themselves in a house of twenty rooms without a servant at their bidding. Every shop was closed against them. Even the coolies who each morning collected the contents of the latrines had deserted, and their husbands had to dispose of the night-soil, as it was politely called. Gervas Bellamy arrived home, harassed and tired, to find his wife standing crying in front of a wood stove she had never seen before. Sarah Mapletoft, expecting a baby at any moment, was discovered by her husband screaming in an empty house, convinced that her labour had started. (The baby did not arrive for several more days.) In the dining-hall in the Fort, protocol was forgotten, nobody bothered to dress for meals, but ate while standing, in their loose Indian-style clothes. The leisurely day-to-day routine had suddenly vanished, and it is ironic to reflect that it was the defection of their servants rather than any other

factor which suddenly aroused the inhabitants of Calcutta to an acute realization that urgent measures were
now a necessity for survival.

The defenders were paraded and divided into six
groups; the three largest were selected to defend the
batteries, a fourth detachment would guard the Fort,
twenty-four men under the command of young Ensign
Piccard were detailed to proceed to Perrin's Redoubt, a
small blockhouse at the extreme north of Black Town
where the Maratha Ditch was (in theory, anyway)
crossed by a bridge and which, according to spies,
would be the Nabob's first objective. A sixth force of
forty men under Lieutenant Blagg was to be kept in
reserve to rush to the defence of any hard-pressed
sector.

O'Hara proved a tower of strength, and a substantial
number of coolies, lured by the promise of extra pay,
were persuaded to remain and worked hastily under his
direction building the three main batteries, while the
main roads, leading north, east and south out of White
Town were blocked by heavy wooden palisades six feet
high. O'Hara's coolies dug trenches twelve feet wide
and nine feet deep across the roads, throwing the earth
against the palisades to form breastworks. Across The
Park the ornamental shrubs were uprooted and a long
straight ditch began to yawn from north to south. Oxen
and horses were set in motion trundling cannon along
The Avenue to the east battery at the corner of Rope
Walk. Bullock carts were requisitioned to bring the
powder from the magazine near the burying-ground to
the Fort, causing chaos on the south road when the troops
discovered that the dusty cart track, which had served
well enough for civilian excursions to The Park or to the
office, was now full of pot-holes which caused axles to
break and wheels to be torn off.

The noise and bustle of military activity must have been infectious. The passive days of uncertainty had gone and for the first time there was something positive to do. The civilians, especially the young writers who were delighted to escape the drudgery of copying or translating, started learning the rudiments of war on the parade-ground and found it a refreshing change to handle a musket instead of a quill. Few had the time or inclination to reflect on the future. This was the glamorous side of war before the shots were exchanged and the dead left unburied. And if they did have any qualms—well, as they no doubt told one another, there was always the Fort. A few older men might have complained about its inadequate defences, but the Fort was the Fort and it would stand for ever. To the young, confident and supremely certain of their superiority to the natives, as they trained on the parade-ground for the first time in their lives, Fort William must have seemed a symbol of power and impregnability, of everything that England stood for.

There was work for the women, too. Records agree that there were about seventy women and forty children in White Town. Under Lady Russell (who would have made an admirable sergeant-major), every woman was set to work filling sacks with cotton waste to heighten the parapet walls and fill in the gun embrasures—which only now were found to be so large that they offered little protection to the gun-crews. Huddled in groups under the arches facing the parade-ground, they filled the sacks one by one as the men waited to take them up the stone steps to the east curtain.

Something had to be done about the children—if only to release the mothers for work. They were installed at first in one of the 'open rooms' near the Black Hole, so as to be close to their mothers who were working in the arcades. Anna Bellamy and Mary Carey were put in charge, for the native servants had gone and they were the only nursemaids available. Mary Carey apparently had a gentle way with children and she sent for Janniko the fiddler to keep the babies amused.

But already time was running dangerously short. By the morning of June 11 spies arriving in Calcutta reported that forward elements of the Nabob's army had crossed the river at Krishnagar, little more than fifty miles north of the city, 'with a great number of cannon, elephants, camels and horses'. It was on this day that Drake decided to have Omichand imprisoned, an act which was to have far-reaching consequences.

It is a complicated story. A few days earlier, Coja Wajid, the Armenian trader to whom the Nabob had addressed his angry letter, had sent an agent to see Drake, suggesting that the Governor write a polite letter of appeasement to the Nabob. Coja Wajid had already drafted this letter and it is a fact that Drake copied it and handed it over to the agent. Whether it ever reached the Nabob we do not know.

The same agent had brought Coja Wajid's warning to Drake that it was Omichand who had encouraged the Nabob to attack Calcutta as a revenge for the manner in which the British had curtailed his financial activities. It is hard to say whether or not this news was true, but Drake apparently took no direct action. He did, however, issue strict instructions that all strangers entering Calcutta should be searched more diligently, and during a routine inspection of a *budgerow* (a small boat) two letters addressed to Omichand were found. They had come, without doubt, from the Nabob's camp and Drake ordered the immediate arrest of Omichand and Kissendass. Ensign Charles Smith with twenty men was detailed to surround the merchant's house on The Avenue and search it after the arrest had been made.

At first all went peacefully. Smith marched up to the front gate of the compound as Bellamy was conducting a service in St Anne's Church, which stood almost next door to Omichand's house. He was received politely by a servant, and when he announced his mission, Omichand offered no resistance. Stony-faced and impassive, he waddled to his special out-size carriage, his enormous body quivering with every step. Kissendass followed. There was no violence, no protests. Perhaps Omichand had been expecting arrest and hardly spoke while he and his companion were driven away to the Fort.

The minute the gate of the compound closed behind him, however, Omichand's private troops opened fire. Smith and his men ran for cover, gaining safety outside the compound wall.

Inside the church a hymn had just ended when musket-fire shattered the silence. The dozen or so women in the congregation doubtless thought the Nabob had arrived and Bellamy could do little to stop them panicking. Some ran for the stairs leading to the bell-tower. Sarah Mapletoft promptly fainted, though Mrs Mackett, who was also expecting a child at any moment, stayed in her pew.

They waited, terrified, but there was no more shooting and finally one or two of the more courageous peeped out to find everything quiet, though there were rather more troops on The Avenue than usual. Perhaps, thought Ensign Smith, the shooting had been a mistake, but when he gingerly pushed open the compound door, a dozen shots sang through the hot air, thudding into the heavy wood.

Smith wisely decided to settle down and await orders or events. He might have wondered why Omichand's troops opened fire after their master had so quietly agreed to his arrest, but he was not to know the gruesome reason. Omichand's troops had been ordered to keep out the British from the compound until his chief foot-man, Jaggernath Singh, had killed the women of the harem.

Many men in the Fort were now to witness the ghastly scene. The sound of shooting must have drawn them to the east curtain, where some had a clear view of Omi-chand's compound. The footman was leading a proces-sion to the edge of a small coconut-grove. Thirteen women and three children followed him in single file. When they reached the palms they stood in a line with a quiet dignity and submission. There was no warning of what was to follow. Without hesitation, the first woman in the line stepped forward and tore her dress from her breasts. The footman drew a dagger from his sash and stabbed her in the heart. She made no sound as she slumped to the ground, and the next woman stepped forward. One by one they moved out of the line as the horrifying ritual proceeded. If there were any shouts from startled watchers in the Fort or the bell-tower of the church, Singh took no notice. In a few minutes it was all over. Then, expressionless, Singh held the dagger high and plunged it into his chest.

When Ensign Smith eventually led his sickened troops past the corpses and into the house, Omichand's troops had fled. Searching the house, they found enough fire-arms to fill two small rooms, proof enough of Omichand's guilt. Smith left the bodies in the compound, assuming they were all dead, but in fact Singh, who had so bravely slaughtered sixteen women and children, had lacked the courage at the last moment to thrust the dagger deep enough into himself. He was gravely wounded but sufficiently alive to play one more important role.

In itself the slaughter in Omichand's garden might have excited no great attention in a harsh country where death was commonplace. But it had a profound effect on the Hindu women. They had seen (or, perhaps worse, their friends had) what could happen to them. Who could doubt that any woman falling into the hands of the Moors would suffer a fate even worse?

At this time there were still over a hundred thousand people left in Black Town, and the British, desperately needing all the labour they could get, were doing everything to prevent them fleeing. The servants of White Town (being more sophisticated) might have gone, but it was much more important to prevent an even greater exodus, since it took two thousand coolies, for example, to transport the powder from the magazine to the Fort. With the inducement of extra pay, the British were holding on to their native help, but only just. Then came the massacre in Omichand's compound, and to the thousands of women in Black Town the message was starkly apparent: if they wanted to save their lives, they had better get out while there was still time. As a direct result of Singh's action, the evacuation, which the British hoped they had checked, started all over again.

The myth of British supremacy was crumbling around the Hindus anyway; its decline was evident in the scared faces of the white women, in the short tempers and the fact that the 'hatmen' no longer bothered to wear their hats. The badge of esteem had been ripped off and beneath it, for the patient, suffering Hindu women to see, were men and women, mortal like themselves. And now this. That night another thirty thousand swept out of Black Town in a flood.

By June 13 the Nabob's forward troops had reached Baraset, a bare fifteen miles north of Calcutta. By the next evening ten thousand were camped on the other side of the Maratha Ditch and the roll of their drums and the lights of their fires reached the Fort itself.

The barricades were ready; the officers had been selected to man each of the three vital batteries. That night spies brought Drake the news that the Nabob intended to attack Perrin's Redoubt at first light the following morning. Preparations were rapidly put in hand. Ensign Piccard and his force were already manning the Redoubt and now Drake ordered Captain Hague of the *Prince George* to sail up-river and lend support with his guns.

The order went out for all European women to seek refuge in the Fort. It was still safe to walk about White Town, and throughout the evening women carried their pitiful bundles of private belongings from houses they would never see again, dodging the powder-trains that cluttered the roads, the officers galloping, the troops swearing, the Indians fleeing from the town.

In that last chaotic evening before the fighting started none had time to realize that this was much more than a skirmish between a stupid Governor and an arrogant Prince. The moment of history is hard to capture while it is being enacted, but this moment marked the end of one epoch and the prelude to another. Few of the hurrying women had time to reflect that even if the Nabob were defeated, it would be only at the cost of profound change. This was a turning-point in history. Nothing could ever be the same again.

CHAPTER THREE

Battle in the Sun

Wednesday, June 16

The method by which the Nabob had captured Cossimbazar may have shown some guile but there was to be
nothing subtle about his attack on Perrin's Redoubt.
Believing it the easiest place where his elephants and
cannon could cross the Maratha Ditch, he merely
ordered four thousand of his best troops, supported by
cannon hidden in the jungle, to overwhelm it. His spies
had informed him that the Redoubt was nothing more
than a square box constructed of *pucca* (the locally made
building material), with embrasures for seven guns,
loopholes for muskets, and barely large enough to hold a
couple of dozen men. To his uncomplicated mind it
must have seemed a simple objective for successive waves
of troops, who would attack regardless of losses until
the defenders were overwhelmed by fatigue, shortage of
powder or sheer weight of numbers.

There was no necessity for concealment on either side.
The Ditch was there, the Redoubt was there, it had to
be assaulted, it had to be defended. It presented one of
those classical set-pieces so beloved by early Indian captains (though perhaps their pleasure was not wholly
shared by the cannon-fodder they employed), and it was
much more like a contest than a battle, in which each

side, separated by a hundred yards or so, merely waited for the opening move.

It is difficult to understand why the Nabob chose to attack the only spot along the whole length of the Ditch which was defended by a fort. There was supposed to be a bridge of sorts there, but it must have long since rotted away. The Ditch was twelve feet wide, but it meandered for miles round the edge of Black Town, and as many of the inhabitants had fled, one would have thought it much easier for the Nabob's foot-soldiers to cross at any one of a score of undefended places where the Ditch was half filled with mud and rubble. And as the whole British plan was based on the defence of set points, no troops could have been spared to repulse an attack by superior forces so far distant from the Fort.

A curious mental stupor seems to have shrouded the minds of the Nabob's generals during the early stages of the siege and many of their actions seem unaccountable in retrospect. Was it really possible that the Nabob believed Perrin's to be the only place where the Ditch could be breached? His spies had entered Calcutta with apparent ease. Why had they not told him that the Ditch had never been completed? It was common knowledge in Calcutta. One can only assume that men like Omichand deliberately preferred to mislead the Nabob by exaggerating the strength of Calcutta's defences in the hope that such misleading intelligence would thwart Siraj-Uddaula of a victory that could only mean the ruination of trade.

A hundred questions remain unanswered. The Nabob, whose large forces could have crossed the Ditch at a dozen places simultaneously, established bridgeheads, and then set about building bridges to get his cannon across, deliberately chose to attack the Redoubt. Though his defeat there had no bearing on the fate of Calcutta, the result of the battle is fascinating historically, for it illustrates how a handful of Europeans were able to withstand continuous assaults by an enemy who outnumbered them fifty to one but had to attack across open ground. It also proves how right O'Hara had been in suggesting that the British should demolish the houses of White Town and defend Fort William only, thus depriving the Indians of any cover.

The Redoubt was set back about a hundred yards from the Ditch, close to the river which, as one looked ahead, lay on the left. The ground directly in front of its walls had at one time been Calcutta's most fashionable pleasure garden until the newly created Park's convenient proximity to the Fort brought about its decline, since when it had degenerated into a dusty, bedraggled wilderness. Where it ended was the Ditch, and beyond that the jungle. Behind the Redoubt a rough but straight road spanned the two miles to the Fort.

About one o'clock on the Wednesday morning the Nabob's troops started moving into the palm-groves and jungle without any effort at secrecy or concealment, and for the rest of the night their torches were visible and their kettle-drums could be plainly heard, drowned occasionally by the heavy crashing of the elephants bringing up the cannon.

Inside the Redoubt Francis Piccard and twenty-five men waited for the dawn, the men sitting or sleeping on the floor of smooth plastered mud littered with powder-kegs and boxes, canisters of water, stocks of cannon-balls. In one corner a small fire was kept going on which from time to time food was heated.

Ensign Piccard was twenty-four, a freckle-faced man with a thatch of red hair; his sergeant was Peter Carey of the militia. Ralph Thoresby, a twenty-three-year-old volunteer, was the only other Englishman in the garrison,

which consisted of Portuguese or Dutch half-caste
mercenaries.

The attack was expected at dawn and Piccard's orders
were to defend the Redoubt to the last man. The *Prince
George* had sailed up-river and Captain Hague, the
skipper, was already in place to bombard the enemy
when he knew their positions. Lieutenant Blagg with
forty men was waiting in the Fort two miles away to lend
assistance when required.

One of the few intelligent decisions ever taken by
Drake (if indeed it was his decision) had been to warn
Piccard that he must fight alone (with the *Prince George*)
during the entire morning, and he made it clear he was
not ready to commit Blagg's men too soon. He must
have based this decision on the knowledge that the
Indians never fought from noon to three, and indeed considered an enemy beneath contempt if he was ill-mannered
enough to ignore the traditional siesta. Therefore if
Piccard was able to hold out during the morning, his men
would be assured of a respite at noon. During the lull
Blagg would move his reinforcements up unknown to the
Nabob, so that when the attack began again, the Indians
would be suddenly faced with fresh troops. When one
reads of the high-level conferences, complicated battle
instructions and troop movements that nowadays mark
even a minor engagement, this local 'siesta rule' may seem
almost incredible and Drake's plan too simple to deceive
the most inexperienced commander, but in fact it was
admirably suited to the times.

It did, however, have one possible flaw. If the Moors
attacked at, say, six a.m., could Piccard's men humanly
be expected to have the staying-power to fight on in the
deadly heat for six hours? It seems impossible, and perhaps they could not have done so, but in fact the battle
was not joined at dawn as everyone expected.

When daylight came with its usual magnificent extravagance, every man in the Redoubt was at his post. Piccard had posted two men to each of the seven cannon embrasures, leaving Carey and a corporal free to move wherever the fighting was hottest. A drill was improvised so that those with muskets would double up at the loopholes. Thus, when the first man had fired, he would step aside and reload while a second man took his place. (It was a complicated operation to reload a musket, while the most brilliant gun-team could not reload a cannon in less than eleven minutes.) Piccard himself would direct operations from a stone platform built with a loophole against the inside of the front wall, from which he had an uninterrupted view of the battlefield ahead.

The garrison waited expectantly but the dawn passed. Odd noises of another hot tropical day began to break the silence—mynah birds chattered, a few monkeys loped across to the Ditch, long-tailed parrots flew away screeching. But not a sound came from the enemy. The sun was already high, the day was already advanced, and Piccard began to feel worried; life in Bengal, warlike or peaceful, always followed such pre-ordained rules that men were invariably astonished (as Watts had been) when those rules were broken. The Indians always attacked at dawn, it was common knowledge; but as the waiting became intolerable and Piccard looked for the hundredth time at his heavy pocket-watch in its shagreen case, he discovered it was nearly eight o'clock.

Already the heat was suffocating and the strain of waiting must have been nerve-racking. One can imagine Piccard praying for some event to break the ominous tension, even a shot to disturb the calm that seemed to hang around them all as every pair of eyes, heavy from fitful sleep, stared at the hundred yards of sun-soaked dust in front of them, the flat, dun ground dancing with moving, shimmering air.

Piccard was not to know until later that the delay had been deliberately planned by Roy Doolub, one of the Nabob's most astute commanders, in the hope of breaking the nerve of the defenders. He had carefully arranged for Drake's spies to learn that he intended to attack at dawn, knowing that to the men in the Redoubt the strain of waiting on the alert for hours would prove a burden so intolerable that it must affect their morale, ensuring, he hoped, a cheaper victory. Unlike the Nabob, Roy Doolub was reluctant to incur heavy losses. The army was already seething with discontent. Many men had not been paid for months. More serious, the majority of the foot-soldiers, often conscripted against their will, still had a healthy respect for the white man's superior fighting power and were convinced they would be slaughtered. Roy Doolub's tactics were designed to raise his troops' morale as much as to gain a victory, and it was unfortunate for this highly intelligent officer, as well as for the eight hundred Indians now about to die, that for once the English displayed a little initiative and guile.

Roy Doolub's tactics came strangely near success, for by ten o'clock Piccard's men were on the verge of panic. The waiting, the invisible foe, the eerie silence, the complete lack of action, was something that puzzled and daunted the Dutch and Portuguese. Soon they were openly demanding to be sent back to the Fort; the heat was enough to make several faint; one Dutchman was heard to cry out that any fight, even if it meant death, was preferable to this intolerable waiting. Eventually Piccard, who was feeling the strain himself, agreed to send a runner the two miles to Fort William, as much for his own sake as to appease the men. The unexpected silence must be causing worry and consternation in the

Fort. Perhaps it crossed his mind that by now they might even imagine his post had been silently wiped out in the night.

But the messenger was never sent. A few minutes after ten o'clock Roy Doolub launched his attack, after an overture fearful enough to make the bravest man quail. One minute there was silence, the next a terrifying sound sent chills through every man in the Redoubt. Forgotten were their grumbles. Out of the jungle one lonely voice pierced the air with a wail that started at the bottom of the scale and then slowly climbed, holding the top note for perhaps thirty eerie seconds. To every man who lived through the battle of Perrin's Redoubt, this must have been the most terrifying experience of his life. Suddenly it stopped for a split second, then every man among the enemy in the jungle, as though he had waited for the pitch to be given with a tuning-fork, screamed as one, and hundreds of Indians, pennants waving, streamed out of the palm-groves in a line more than two hundred yards long.

While the British levelled their muskets, the Indians took up positions, some lying, some kneeling, others standing behind them, all with no cover. There must have been five hundred in the first wave. Piccard had twenty-two muskets.

All thoughts of mutiny instantly vanished. The long silence had ended, the element of the unknown had disappeared, the tension had snapped. This was something that each man, however badly trained, could understand. Men they could see, men they could fight, men they could kill. They actually cheered hysterically, no doubt impelled by the strange exuberance that often infects men when the moment of action arrives. Nobody apparently waited for orders, and from every loophole a musket cracked.

One can picture that moment, with the Indian line so tightly bunched that not a man in the Redoubt could miss. As the reserve musketeers fired the second volley, one cannot help being reminded, however macabre it sounds, of a fairground booth where the targets fall backwards and one is rewarded with a china vase for three successful shots.

The Indian musket-fire was ragged and harmless, but the garrison's elation was quickly shattered as St Jacques's cannon crashed out from their hidden sites in the jungle. The first three balls whistled overhead, but with the fourth the French gunner scored a direct hit and the Redoubt was immediately filled with acrid smoke, dust, rubble, and the moans of wounded men.

The Indians now began to yell and scream in triumph, and we have it that Piccard went to an embrasure to see why Captain Hague of the *Prince George* had not found the range of the enemy cannon. Hague, however, had other ideas. While some of his seamen were pinpointing the orange flashes of the Indian cannon, his two best gunners were waiting, portfires ready, by two cannon previously trained on the Ditch itself.

Hague was aware that at the first sign of success the Moors would be unable to control themselves. He was right, for now that the Redoubt was hit they made a headlong dash for the Ditch, firing wildly as they ran, jumping down into it and up the opposite bank to reach the open ground for the final assault on the Redoubt. At exactly the right moment Hague's two guns opened fire. The men in the Redoubt heard the roar slam across the river. The effect was devastating.

Every man in the garrison except Piccard was ramming home charges or firing. He alone witnessed what happened: the flashes before the roar, the geysers of dust swirling into the air. He saw the moving figures by the river, some kneeling to fire, some standing, some scrambling over the lip of the Ditch, suddenly blown away. One moment the attackers were there, the next the air was alive with dust and flying bodies, arms and legs without bodies, all blown into the sky. Then the dust turned into a cloud and he could see nothing, only hear the screams of agony and fear. Over the river a thick fog of black smoke hung in the still, hot air. Automatically Piccard looked at his watch. It was twenty-five minutes past ten.

Unaware of the slaughter, the men inside the Redoubt still stumbled cursing over one another, blinded by smoke. The enemy's direct hit had pierced the north wall, killing one man and wounding two more, while the dusty sunlight blazed in like a flame through the gap the ball had torn. Nobody, however, had time even to make the wounded comfortable before a fresh wave of Moors launched a second attack out of the jungle, hundreds of them running swiftly towards the Ditch, apparently undeterred by the bodies sprawled in their path.

Hague had had no time to reload (he seems to have made a serious error in firing both guns at the first wave), but Piccard acted with great coolness. He ordered his men to hold their fire until the Indians tried to climb up the near side of the Ditch; he had already trained two of his seven cannon to cover the ground immediately in front of the Fort. Now, as the first heads appeared over the Ditch, muskets and cannon opened fire, but so many men came flooding on to the breathless stretch of land in front of them, the fire was not heavy enough to stop the rush. On the Indians came. Some carried muskets, others scimitars, sabres, bayonets, all twinkling in the sun.

The British musketeers fired with magnificent discipline. Only one voice could be heard above the din as the master-gunner yelled, 'Load! Rod! Home! Return!

Cap!' Then 'Fire!' The men would fire as one, step back, the second rank would move into position and again the master-gunner would cry the complicated orders. For a moment or two it looked as though Piccard had stopped them, but then another enemy cannon tore through the Redoubt's walls, knocking out one of the guns. In the resulting chaos some of the Indians managed to reach the walls and Piccard ran to one loop-hole and to his astonishment saw a brown hand gripping the sill. A soldier brushed past him and sliced it off with one blow of his sword. Men pointed their muskets downwards before shooting; others waited until the Moors were close enough to be bayoneted. Three Indians ran round the Redoubt and tried to force their way through the only entrance-slit at the rear, but were driven off after hand-to-hand fighting in which one resourceful Portuguese grabbed a burning portfire from a cannon and thrust it into a screaming Indian face.

Meantime, new waves were pouring out of the jungle. Hague had now had time to reload, but his guns were trained on the jungle and Ditch and the bulk of the Indians were now half-way across Perrin's Garden. This was the moment Piccard had been waiting for. He himself dropped the burning portfire to the torch-hole and waited for the shivering air to burst and crack his ear-drums as the first ball shrieked into the midst of the Moors barely fifty yards away.

Those at the loopholes had an instant's vision of the carnage, the scrabbling figures, the bodies and flesh, the heads and entrails, the arms and disconnected feet, the spurting blood. One man, his leg blown off, tried to stand, holding up the Nabob's flag in a pathetic gesture of defiance. But his remaining leg gave way beneath him and soon he was crawling round in circles, still clutching the banner.

The centre of the line of Indians had been devastated, but it seemed as though those on both wings who escaped hardly realized what had happened. It was as though they were hypnotized into advancing whatever the cost. Suddenly, however, Piccard saw through the haze one man—only one—falter. It was probably a single moment of fear which in the noise and turmoil would have gone unnoticed, yet that split second was sufficient. Every man seemed instinctively to sense that hesitation. The faltering increased and suddenly the ragged line dissolved and crumpled. Almost before Piccard could shout the news to the garrison, the Indians were pouring back like a cataract, falling, scrambling, losing their balance, tumbling over one another into the Ditch which provided not an inch of shelter and where hundreds died as Captain Hague poured out streams of orange fire from the *Prince George.*

Piccard climbed down into the dust from his platform. The Redoubt was now a horrifying sight. The second cannon shot had torn another hole above a forward embrasure. The gun beside it was wrecked and three bodies lay over the still-hot barrel. A portfire blazed in a corner. A third shot had fallen through the roof. Every man was so black with grime that Piccard at first did not recognize Carey when he spoke to him. There was bad news. Thoresby had been killed, the first of the Company's servants to fall. He had been shot through the heart, and Piccard and Carey pulled the boy's body into a corner and covered it as decently and quickly as they could before attending to more urgent matters. Piccard himself had been wounded in the head, but it seems that he had no idea how it had been caused, nor did he feel any pain. He made a rough bandage with part of a dead man's shirt, and as he looked at the dead and wounded lying in the litter of powder-kegs, twisted wood and iron, the spilled powder, the smashed cannon, he must have wondered how much longer the Redoubt could hold out.

Yet there could be no retreat. This was not a question of where their duty lay; every instinct must have urged them to cling to the frail protection of four walls, or what remained of them. Once out in the open they would have been overwhelmed and massacred.

No one seems to be certain how many more attacks were launched on the Redoubt before noon. Some say two, others three. The defenders were so dazed they fought on like robots, hardly realizing what they were doing or what was happening around them; but after the second slaughter the Indian attacks were on a much reduced scale. Possibly Roy Doolub was regrouping for a massive assault later in the day; perhaps he hoped the British would ask for quarter. St Jacques's cannon scored one more direct hit but only one man was wounded, and it seems that the musketeers were kept occupied by small, sporadic raids in which they suffered no losses.

Then, as suddenly as it had started, the clamour of the fighting ceased. What an incredibly dramatic moment it must have been for the British, exhausted, hungry, desperately thirsty, staggering around, their minds fogged, unable to escape the stench of the dead, already swelling in the heat; what a moment when they suddenly realized that nobody was shooting at them any more. The noon siesta. The vultures, which had been frightened by the noise, had instinctively returned and were now circling high over the field of battle, but none of the defenders was able to explain afterwards what that electric moment felt like or how it arrived. It was noon, that was all that mattered, and the lull was probably as acceptable to Roy Doolub as it was to Ensign Piccard.

Back in the Fort where the gunfire had been plainly

heard (no doubt with much relief), Drake decided to send messengers to Piccard and Hague acquainting them with a change of plan. Originally it had been intended to send Lieutenant Blagg directly to the Redoubt, but early in the morning Captain Grant and Holwell had somehow persuaded Manningham to adopt a more cunning manœuvre. (They had approached Manningham knowing he would be able to influence Drake more easily than they.) Accordingly Blagg had set off about ten o'clock with fifty men, an eighteen-pounder and two brass field-pieces with the idea of veering to the east before reaching the Redoubt and advancing into the Bagh Bazaar, the great market of Black Town. A moderately good road branched off from the main road that led from Calcutta to Perrin's Garden, and once inside the fringes of the Bazaar, where he would be to some extent sheltered and certainly hidden, Blagg would have a clear field of fire for his guns, which would not only command the Ditch in front of the Redoubt but would also give clear shooting into the Indian positions on the other side.

Because of the immense trouble of hauling the eighteen-pounder over the bad roads, he had had to start early. This ancient but effective piece of iron weighed twenty-seven tons and normally needed thirty yoke of oxen to drag it, but as nobody could muster so many, a makeshift team of oxen and horses, with soldiers heaving at the wheels, managed to pull the gun to the Bazaar— a distance, including the detour, of over two miles—in four hours.

Two messengers were now dispatched, one rowing a budgerow up-river to Captain Hague, the other on horseback to Ensign Piccard, to instruct both to open fire with every gun they could at two-fifteen. If Blagg could open fire at the same time, the Indians would be under bombardment from three sides.

Captain Hague received his instructions with relish. The *Prince George*, though in theory a merchant ship, bore much more resemblance to a man-o'-war in both design and equipment. She was pierced for twenty nine-pounders on her gun-deck, and carried six six-pounders on her quarter-deck. She displaced 498 tons (carefully calculated at the time of construction to evade carrying the chaplain obliged by law to sail on all vessels of 500 tons or more). Hague was already highly delighted with his morning's performance, but the prospect of taking the war into the enemy's camp rather than merely supporting Piccard pleased him even more.

The other messenger reached the Redoubt shortly after twelve-thirty to find almost all the defenders, other than Piccard and two sentries, asleep. The smoke had cleared, but now the shattered roof and walls offered virtually no shelter against the burning sun, and men had crawled into corners of shade and fallen asleep wherever they could.

Piccard had tried to bring some order out of the shambles. The dead had been dragged behind the Redoubt, and though no time could be spared to bury them, they had been covered. The wrecked guns had been hauled out to make more room, and as soon as the messenger arrived, everyone was awakened, given a stiff tot of arrack, and put to work preparing the three remaining cannon in the forward embrasures.

As they struggled to get the cannon into position (even a six-pounder weighed nine tons), a new excitement surged through the tired defenders. Cheering, singing, sometimes laughing, they carried the case-shot filled with bits of metal and grape, and stacked them beside each cannon. Powder-kegs, rammers, sponges, ladles, were all placed handy. Grunting men forced wedges under the cannon to elevate the line of fire. Stripped to the waist, they started to load. First the match or fuse, pushed through the firing end until it touched the base of the barrel, then the powder, pushed hard with the leather-tipped ramrod; then the wadding —anything they could lay hands on, paper, wool, sawdust—all rammed home tightly; and finally the ball itself so that all was prepared for the master-gunner to light the match with the portfire.

Away on their right as they worked, the men could see the squalid tumbledown shacks of the Bazaar quite clearly. Somewhere inside the dark shadows Blagg must be waiting. To their left they could make out figures strolling, nonchalantly it seemed, along the safe, secure decks of the *Prince George*. In front of them the vultures had wheeled down from the blue bowl of the sky and were fighting over the corpses rotting in the sun. Every now and again the slightest hint of a breeze wafted the terrible stench of putrefying bodies into the Redoubt and men would vomit where they stood. They worked without pause until two o'clock before Piccard was satisfied.

A quarter of an hour later the stillness of the hot afternoon was shattered by a bombardment from the *Prince George*. Hague had been able to bring eight of his guns to bear on the Moors' camp and he now began firing a gun every three minutes, in order to give his men time to reload and thus keep up a continuous fire. Piccard opened with his first cannon almost at the same moment, then carried on firing at six-minute intervals to give his gunners time to sponge the guns and douse them with water to cool the hot iron. Then from the Bazaar came the welcome heavy grumble of Blagg's eighteen-pounder, followed by the sharper bark of the two field-pieces.

Between them the British were now firing fourteen cannon at the rate of one almost every minute.

In the Indian lines it must have seemed as though the firing was continuous; cannon-balls were now plunging in on them from three sides. Taken completely by surprise, the Indians cowered on the ground in terror. The din was terrific as ball after ball crashed through the jungle. Within a few minutes several small fires started burning in the trees. The Indians were so astounded they never ventured to reply.

The panting, sweating men cheered as they saw debris soar into the air. Nobody knew exactly what had been hit or which gun had found such an important target. How long the bombardment lasted nobody has recorded, for in the confusion, all count of time seems to have been lost. The firing probably went on for the best part of an hour, and throughout the entire time not a single answering shot came from St Jacques's guns in the jungle.

It seemed inexplicable, for the French-directed artillery was both accurate and well-trained. It was only later that the British discovered a lucky shot had smashed two French cannon, blown up several kegs of powder (probably the bits and pieces they saw flying in the air), and killed three senior officers, two of them French. Captured spies later admitted that Roy Doolub had been thunderstruck when he realized he was being attacked on a third front; and though the Indian accounts are sketchy, they make it clear that the ordinary soldiers, who had suffered such grievous and gruesome losses in the forenoon, were terrified to the point where nothing could force them to action. Shouts, threats, the lash, would not budge men so far demoralized they could not understand the frantic orders nor even feel the rain of blows. They sat there, according to one report, dumb and uncomprehending, among the dead and the untended wounded.

Suddenly two of the elephants broke their leg-chains and, trumpeting madly, crashed out of the jungle and lumbered at full speed towards the Ditch, where they lost their footing and tumbled in amid the dead and wounded.

The Indians in the jungle could stand the cannon-fire no longer. Hundreds flooded out of the trees, running towards the Ditch, desperate only to reach open ground. Some, apparently stunned with disaster, ran or fell into the Ditch, where they were trampled to death.

It was the turning-point of the battle. Piccard ordered the musketeers to prepare to fire. Blagg's field-pieces, easily manœuvrable, sent two balls crashing among the Indians. Those in the Redoubt could see the astonished faces of the enemy, twisting in surprise, looking to the Bazaar, as though they could not believe there was yet another invisible enemy. When Blagg's muskets fired from one quarter and Piccard's from another, the Indians as one man bolted back to the jungle—not for their camps, but anywhere, anywhere so long as it was away from the English.

It was the end of the battle for Perrin's Redoubt, and the Nabob admitted later that out of four thousand picked troops, eight hundred had been killed. The English lost five soldiers in the Redoubt, including Thoresby, with another five wounded. Four Europeans were killed on the *Prince George*.

The Nabob never again attacked from that quarter. There was no need.

CHAPTER FOUR

The Great Fire of Calcutta

Thursday, June 17

At this time the Nabob had set up his headquarters in Omichand's house, which stood on the edge of the Maratha Ditch two miles east of Fort William. Normally Omichand had used this four-bedroomed wooden building surrounded by pleasure gardens as a summer residence in hot weather. At this time and distance we do not know whether the Nabob had merely occupied the house or whether the wily Omichand had placed it at his disposal. But it seems that its ostentatiously vulgar furniture so displeased the Nabob that he ordered every stick of it thrown out into the compound and replaced it with his own, borne on the camels from Murshidabad.

Around his headquarters and stretching far back behind the Ditch, avenues of coloured tents marked the presence of his forces for miles across the plain. The Nabob's own tent—set up in Omichand's garden—was constructed of scarlet material embroidered with gold. Sixty feet long and thirty feet in height, it rested on poles as thick as the masts of ships. At either end flags drooped listlessly in the hot air. There were flags on hundreds of other tents also—yellow, blue, vermilion, or even woven into broad striped bands of canvas. The tents were grouped into avenues, where privacy for the

Nabob's senior officers, aides, and dependent rajahs was assured by means of brightly coloured canvas screens partitioning off each tent from its neighbour. Sentries stood guard at each tent, looking often no doubt towards the impressive path which led to the Nabob's tent which was lined with carpets, secured against any unexpected gale which might blow in from the river by gold pillars and heavy ornaments encrusted with jewels.

The historians are less communicative about the comforts and morale of the rank and file of the Nabob's army. These rows of tents which housed his officers were a world of their own, in which the Nabob alone had a hundred personal servants, and the French officers had brought along thirty-eight barrels of wine and a complement of unattached ladies. Markedly different were the conditions of the ragamuffin foot-soldiers, who possessed no tents and were even in straitened circumstances for food. Little forethought seems to have been given to the wounded, who were probably regarded as an unfortunate encumbrance, and the dispirited remnants of the army which stumbled back wounded or unwounded through the night from Perrin's Redoubt were hardly likely to have received a hero's welcome from a despot never slow to demonstrate his severe displeasure. 'His army,' says one French report, 'marched unwillingly, his people murmured against him and said that he was taking them to be butchered and that they could never capture the place.'

Even the Nabob must have been aware of this alarmingly low morale, for the early hours of Thursday found him in consultation with Coja Wajid. The Armenian, who had been sent for on the pretext of discovering what he knew about conditions inside the Fort, arrived about one a.m. and it was not long before the Nabob was requesting his observations on the troops' morale. The atmosphere was oppressive rather than dramatic and Coja Wajid, thrust into this unwelcome role, must have felt terrified, for he was a wretched little man with none of Omichand's fearless dignity.

It must have been a curious meeting. Roy Doolub attended but never said a word. The Nabob's senior commanders were equally glum. No one could conceal the extent of the rout at Perrin's Redoubt, and soon, under the Nabob's persistent questioning, it seems that Coja Wajid confirmed the rumours, as did several of the senior officers, for the Nabob is recounted to have rounded on one of them crying, 'I do not doubt that thou art afraid, and I am not astonished for thou art a Bengali coward.' Then, turning to Coja Wajid, he went on in a voice possibly intended for Roy Doolub, 'Learn today that we must conquer or die. I am not Aliverdi Khan, nor any of my predecessors. I am Siraj-Uddaula. I do exactly as I please, and it will cost any man his life who dares to suggest anything contrary to my wish or intention.'

His obvious intention to launch a new attack on Perrin's Redoubt was abruptly changed an hour later. Had not Omichand's wounded servant—the man who had butchered the harem—unexpectedly appeared out of the night there is no doubt the Redoubt would have been assaulted again with elephants and cannon, since before that moment not a man in his army suspected they were not facing a wide and continuous ditch.

It is idle yet fascinating to imagine what the outcome of the siege might have been had Omichand's footman plunged his dagger only a quarter of an inch deeper into his chest, for he would have died instantly and history might have been changed. Singh, however, had survived and when he staggered into Omichand's garden at two o'clock that morning, he brought news which caused the Nabob to make a complete change of plan. So it was left to a dying servant to help shape history for the next few decades.

It happened unexpectedly. Coja Wajid had long since departed, and the Nabob was sleeping when he was awakened by noises in his garden. Now, awakening the Nabob was a dangerous undertaking for which a man might easily lose his nose and ears. Roused, he strode furiously to the veranda of the first floor and ordered the culprits thrown into gaol where he would deal with them next morning. At that moment Roy Doolub appeared. There was a man outside, he said, who carried an urgent message from Omichand.

How Singh penetrated to Omichand's garden, how he managed to pass the dozens of guards is a mystery. Presumably when he announced that he bore a message from Omichand he was let through, for this, after all, was his master's garden. He may, too, have known a secret entrance. None the less, it is strange, for Singh was in any case so gravely wounded that he had had to be lifted on to a horse and tied to the saddle for the journey. He was accompanied by another servant, Omrao, and was already dying when he reached the Nabob, who, clad in a short dressing-gown and still very cross, now learned the one vital fact which none of his sycophants had ever told him. The Maratha Ditch, stumbling-block to all his ambitions and dreams, the invincible moat which he believed surrounded Calcutta, had never been finished. After all these years, in which fortunes had been spent in spying and intelligence to no avail, a servant dying from self-inflicted wounds was now telling him the truth.

The news was contained in a letter from Omichand, though when the message was written, nobody knows. It is possible that Omichand, anticipating arrest, had left the message with Singh, but if that had been the case why did Singh try to commit suicide? As with so many bizarre details of the siege, there is no answer.

Omichand's letter revealed that a gap at least a mile wide existed at the south-east end of the Ditch. Even more startling was the news that directly east of the Fort, at the end of a straight road that continued on after The Avenue had petered out, there was a point called the Bread and Cheese Bungalow, where elephants and cannon would be easily able to cross. An assault force, Omichand suggested, might make an attack there while the rest of the army marched round the southernmost point of the Ditch and entered White Town without meeting any serious opposition.

Elated, the Nabob sent for St Jacques, who appeared in a short dressing-gown and a tasselled sleeping-cap. (One story suggests that he was disturbed while participating in some nocturnal frolic, but after the rigours of the previous day's fighting, this is hard to accept, even of a Frenchman.)

Roy Doolub, suspecting a ruse, appears to have expressed doubts as to the veracity of the report, but his suspicion evaporated when the dying Singh ordered his companion Omrao to lead out a party of the Nabob's scouts to ascertain the truth for themselves.

When Singh had been carried away, the Nabob lost no time in making a complete change of plan. He immediately ordered Roy Doolub to move a powerful striking force to the Bread and Cheese Bungalow at daybreak. A diversionary force was to cross the Ditch at the same point, but then make its way to the north battery to prevent the British from concentrating their strongest forces at the east battery, which had been constructed at the corner of The Avenue and Rope Walk. Plainly it would take all day to get the troops into position, but no matter; the British would be unable to stop them forming up.

The main assault was set for the following day, Friday, the eighteenth, an auspicious day in the fasting month of Ramadan, which, as a good Moslem, the Nabob was now rigorously observing. The attack would go in at dawn. Almost as an afterthought the Nabob gave permission to his plunderers to set fire to the great Bazaar the following evening, from where Blagg had attacked. It would teach the inhabitants a lesson.

In a curious manner Drake and Minchin seem almost to vanish from the picture on this last day of feverish preparation. They obviously must have been directing the defences but their actions did not register with those survivors who became chroniclers, and though one hesitates to suggest this (for it is only conjecture), one has the feeling that the garrison racing against time to complete the Fort's preparations virtually ignored them. It was probably intuitive rather than deliberate; time was short, there was a job to do; this was no time for the niceties of protocol, to be more than polite to a governor who was thoroughly disliked.

As for their opinion of Captain Minchin (most likely sulking at the preferment of the civilians), there was not a man who did not agree with Holwell that 'touching the military capacity of our Commandant, I am a stranger. I can only say we are unhappy in his keeping it to himself, if he has any; as neither I, nor I believe anyone else, was witness to any part of his conduct that spoke or bore the appearance of his being the commanding military officer in the garrison.'

The Fort had been stripped for action and O'Hara's engineers, with Leach and his carpenters, had done

everything possible to remedy the appalling defects in
its defences. The news of Ensign Piccard's resounding
victory had put some heart into men who for days now
had been doing the work of coolies in a temperature that
rarely dropped below ninety-four degrees. There was
nothing romantic about that last day, for the heat pressed
down on them like a giant blanket, the air was alive with
the hum of thousands of mosquitoes, and every dark
corner hid rats creeping out of the mud on which the
Fort had been built (and which were as belligerent as the
rats are in Calcutta today).

Long before dawn the women were astir preparing
makeshift breakfasts, though perhaps it was not duty
alone that drove them to this outdoor task, but a desire
to escape from the crowded, dank rooms where sleep was
impossible. The walls of Writers' Row dripped with
condensation. The toilet facilities were hardly adequate
for the handful of apprentices who normally used them.
The change in diet was swiftly producing the first cases
of dysentery, particularly among the children who often
had no changes of clothes. Many women, the sweat
drying on their cumbersome gowns, went unwashed, for
though the Fort had a good water supply, it had to be
harboured for drinking and swilling down the cannon,
and Frankland suggested that the women wash in the
Hoogly. Most Englishwomen were too shy to do so,
but a few did, standing knee-deep side by side with the
Indians, who for centuries had used the river as both
bathroom and lavatory.

By nine a.m. everybody in the Fort was aware that in
less than twenty-four hours the Nabob would launch
his heaviest attack against the east battery. There was
hardly any need for confirmation from the ubiquitous
spies, for all morning the Nabob's new plan was obvious
to the anxious garrison. Cannon were being hauled or

pushed across the Ditch at the Bread and Cheese Bungalow, and by midday teams of oxen were pulling them along the straight track towards the gaol in front of the east battery. From the back of Lady Russell's house sentries could at times plainly see them—each animal decorated with flags or pennants, the oxen heaving, the elephants pushing, the camels lumbering behind, loaded with barrels of powder, cannon-balls and shot.

All morning the enemy marched into position, and though there was no fighting on this day of preparation, before long they came within range of the east battery with its complement of ninety-eight men.

This battery was to be the most vital of all, but by one of those strokes of misfortune which at the time pass unnoticed, it happened to be under the command of Captain Clayton, Minchin's second-in-command, who was if possible even more incompetent than his superior officer. It had never been intended that Clayton should command the east battery. Holwell, already second-in-command of the battery, was a much better choice and the two very brave subalterns, Lieutenant Melchior Lebeaume (another French deserter) and Ensign Carstairs, had both asked for Holwell to command it, even though he was not a professional soldier.

This had been virtually agreed, and it had been decided to leave Clayton with the troops in the Fort when the news came to Manningham's ears. Now Manningham hated Clayton, and since this antipathy was vigorously returned, was determined not to have him with him in the Fort. So Clayton stayed in the battery, and a mutual hatred, which should have been forgotten in the greatest emergency the settlement had ever known, was now ironically to have disastrous consequences for every man and woman in the garrison, and indeed affect the fate of the city itself.

In the midday sun the Fort resounded with the urgent noises of last-minute effort. The parade-ground, usually deserted at this time of day, was alive with moving figures. Cannon-balls, powder-barrels, grape, were still being sorted out, and the ammunition stacked in some sort of order. In one corner, says a report, six armourers laboured all day sharpening the garrison's swords. In another, men sifted dry powder from damp as each barrel arrived from the magazine. Sacks of rice and wheat, enough to withstand a siege of six months, were piled in bulging squares near Writers' Row. On the bastions, working parties prepared the cannon, cursing at fresh evidences of neglect. Many of the six-pounders now about to be used had never been tested, let alone fired. There were insufficient rammers topped with lambswool sponges to clean out the barrels after firing. Lack of water might kill a man within a day or so in this heat; lack of water could finish the Fort in a matter of minutes, and yet there was even a shortage of water canisters, although scores were going to be desperately needed to be carried to each bastion, ready to cool the hot guns after firing.

The men must have worked in a rage of effort, blindly punishing their bodies, for by the afternoon most of the sandbags were in position masking the embrasures. The women had filled over two thousand of the bags, but even these were not enough, and now more than a thousand mattresses had to be carried up from the stores to the east curtain to pad and heighten the miserably thin walls.

Elsewhere, there was an equal tumult of work to be got through. The Avenue leading past St Anne's and the north-south road linking the Fort with the hospital and magazine were choked with galloping officers and creaking bullock-carts, and those coolies who had remained were now heaving the guns and carrying the ammunition to the batteries. Across The Park, sweating bare-chested men had almost finished digging a trench its whole length and at the south-west corner a palisade had been erected and a six-pounder mounted under its cover.

Yet despite the clamour and activity, something seemed to be missing in the streets, though one could not sense at first what it was. The street was noisier, of course, but in a way difficult to explain it also seemed subtly quieter. The overtones were there in the noise and clangour of last-minute preparations, but to the ears of the British, attuned to the special noises of Bengal, the undertones had vanished—the sounds of the Indians themselves; Indians whose sounds had become so familiar over the years that one had hardly noticed them until the moment now when they had ceased. Servants, grooms, shoppers, conjurers, beggars, roundel boys who carried every man's umbrella to shield him against the sun—each had his own peculiar cries and sounds; and now they had all vanished, and the European noises of cries and curses impinged quite differently.

Before dusk, each battery was fully manned. The southern battery, under Captains Buchanan and Mackett, had a complement of ninety-eight personnel; the north, under Captain-Lieutenants Smith and Mapletoft, had sixty-eight men. Lieutenant Blagg's men would again be held in reserve to be rushed to any point where the garrison might be hard pressed.

It was a melancholy prospect; the gaps in the defences were only too apparent; the strength of the garrison was pitiable in mere numbers against the massive army waiting to attack. But the decision to defend Calcutta had been made, and despite a host of initial mistakes the men who now stared out over the makeshift parapets had done all that was humanly possible. As the moon came up, there was little they could do but wait.

Sleep was slow in coming to the Reverend Gervas
Bellamy that night. The cramped rooms in Writers'
Row were stifling, the scuffle of rats worse than in his
own house. Finally he left Dorothy and Anna tossing
fitfully on their pallets and climbed up to the east wall
for some air. He was an old man (for Calcutta) and the
strain was beginning to tell. Had Bellamy lived, he
would probably have written the best account of the
siege, for apparently he was a great talker, and could
discuss the world's problems—which really meant Calcutta's problems—at length over the claret he dis-
pensed so liberally. Increasingly as the years passed,
however, he inclined towards melancholy. He had out-
lived an era; Calcutta had relentlessly squeezed the
energy out of him, and he was unable to adjust himself
to the changes around him. And now, though he was to
fight loyally and bravely, he was already too old for war.

It seems he must have been preoccupied with the fate
of the younger members of the garrison. The death of
Thoresby had made him realize that the youngsters were
now soldiers—boys like Piccard, Blagg, Lushington and
John, his own son—many of whom must now die.
Being the same age as John and lonely, many of them
had become almost part of the family. If Thoresby could
die so easily, what would happen to the others? Particularly John. No man should have a favourite child,
but if anything happened to his youngest son, he prayed
only that he might die by his side.

It was a time when everybody in the settlement brought
their troubles to the parson. Peter Carey had come to
see him before leaving for Perrin's and asked if, in return
for his volunteering for the militia, he might expect some

assurance that Mary would be included in any evacuation plans for the European women. Bellamy had promised he would arrange it, but he knew how difficult it would be were an exception made which would allow even one Eurasian to join the white women. Thomas, too, his eldest son, was a constant worry. At best he was moody and introspective (though with excellent prospects in the export warehouse), but he had become unapproachable, silent and sullen.

It had been a bad day. He had witnessed an ugly incident when the Dutch sergeant, Hedleburgh, had been found drunk and violent. Hedleburgh was a gross brute of a man, a bully and enormously strong, regularly in trouble and the acknowledged leader of the fifty Dutch (or half-Dutch) mercenaries in the garrison. If he always seemed to have more money than could possibly be accounted for from his normal pay, well, in Calcutta it was unwise to enquire into suspicious financial transactions. Too many cupboards hid golden skeletons and one never knew which door would be opened next. However, during the sharp struggle at his arrest, several gold and silver coins had fallen from Hedleburgh's pockets. There was no doubt they came from the Nabob's treasury. The thought that the Fort might harbour a traitor must have upset the simple philosophy of the chaplain more than anything else.

Such thoughts probably crowded his mind as he leaned against the east wall silently looking out over White Town. The time was a little before midnight and a dozen sentries slouched over the parapet. The night was dark except for a thin moon, and he had stood there for perhaps half an hour before noticing something strange. The moon was suddenly blotted out. A thin cloud crossed it, and for one second he entertained the wild hope that the monsoon had arrived early—which would have effectively stopped any thoughts of war, for nobody could fight during the weeks of torrential downpour. But it couldn't be that; the cloud moved too quickly. Another followed it and every star was suddenly obliterated.

It was smoke, thick black smoke darkening the night sky. In a few moments the orange and scarlet glow of flames became visible. The sentries began talking excitedly. Without hesitation, Bellamy stumbled down the stone steps to the parade-ground to wake the Captain of the Guard, who, according to custom, was snoozing in the arcade. It happened to be Tooke (now in the militia), and by the time they had climbed back to the east curtain, Black Town—which stretched two miles to the north-east of the Fort—was a blazing furnace which according to Tooke, 'burnt till morning and, being so very extensive and near, formed a scene too horrible for language to describe'.

Within half an hour the flames which followed their progress had spread from the Bazaar to the northern section of Black Town and those in the Fort could read by their light. Long before the fire, however, a tidal wave of brown bodies had swept into the narrow, twisting, foetid alleys of the Bazaar as more of the Nabob's plunderers flooded hungrily into the Town, hacking down the pitiful shops and thatched huts, or using torches, screaming, yelling, drunk with defiance and burning zeal.

Shopkeepers rising too late from beside their flat wicker baskets of ghee or fruit vanished under thousands of feet. Women were dragged from doorways into the steaming night until they too disappeared as more and more bands of plunderers pressed forward, surging from street to street. Soon the smell of burning flesh mingled with the sharp scent of burning, crackling wood.

If the mud houses refused the flames, sweating, struggling gangs of men piled the stinking ground-floor cubicles with every stick of furniture they could find, and fired that. The slaughter was indiscriminate and carried out with maniacal fury. Learned Brahmins trying to protect their books, shopkeepers with their scales, ironsmiths and potters with their sticks and wheels—all were trapped.

The plunderers stole what they wanted and smashed up everything else. And always they were searching for money. Merchants, who had long since buried their treasure, became their especial prey, and each one who refused to reveal its whereabouts was brutally tortured, usually by being held upside down and having water poured into his nose. If this failed to bring any response, boiling oil would be poured down his throat.

It is said that the Nabob himself at one time galloped into the alleys of Black Town, riding a white charger and hacking his way through the dying, trapped Hindus, but the details of the tortures and sadism of that dreadful night will never be fully known; nor how many people were killed or burned alive, though the number must have run into thousands. Many on the northern and eastern edges of Black Town escaped into the jungle. There was no time to snatch even a pitiful bundle of belongings, nor, in many cases, to search for wives and children.

The fire must have stretched nearly two miles, for the great sprawling ant-heap of Black Town extended, as we have noted, from the perimeter of Calcutta almost to the walls of the European section, and in that part of Black Town nearest to the Fort lived most of the wives and families of the garrison's mercenaries and many of the coolies.

The effect of the fire on these people—to say nothing

of the horrifying stampede of their countrymen—was disastrous. Over a thousand coolies who had remained with the garrison—tempted by triple pay to stay and carry powder to the ramparts and batteries—now contrived to vanish away into the jungle, while as the nearest flames licked their way almost to the compound walls of White Town, thousands of women and children surged towards the big houses nearest the Fort. The helpless garrison could do nothing but stare in horror at the vast holocaust and listen to its dreadful noises as it spread crackling over acre after acre of bone-dry shacks.

Suddenly, sporadic fighting broke out near the east gate. Some of the native militia were demanding refuge for their wives. If this was not granted, they cried, they would refuse to fight. The gate was closed—but then it was forced open again.

Out of Black Town's dozens of tiny alleys north of The Avenue, little trickles of women and children now started appearing, running past the walls of the houses belonging to Omichand, Bellamy and Mapletoft. As though by instinct, they all made for the comparative safety of The Avenue, and before the dazed garrison was aware of what was happening, some of the militia had drawn their swords on officers at the east gate trying to prevent coloured wives and children streaming into the Fort. The few regular troops who rushed to their aid were overwhelmed and pushed roughly aside as the first trickle swelled into a tide. Fighting and screaming, they fought their way to the Fort. The whole Avenue near the Fort was choked with half-crazy Hindus, their wives and children, most of them poor and destitute, but also some rich merchants whose slaves carried large bundles of belongings and dealt mercilessly with the less fortunate who stood in their path.

Any opposition by the garrison was out of the question

as the refugees, framed in the searing light of the fire, virtually stormed the Fort.   Only musket-fire could possibly have arrested their progress, but such desperate measures were unthinkable.   Nothing could stop them bursting through the east gate, scrambling up the stone steps, flooding on to the parade-ground and into every empty cubicle and corner they could discover.

As dawn came up, the Bagh Bazaar was slowly burning itself out.   The garrison could see nothing but smoke curling over the grotesque shadows of the gutted hovels and shops.   The alleyways were thick with grey ash.

Inside the Fort, which at this moment should have been poised to withstand the Nabob's first great assault on White Town, the commanders could only stare in blank dismay at the chaos around them.   This was the moment when the battle for Calcutta was about to be joined, when the last preparations had been made to withstand attack, when the Fort had been stripped for action.   And only now, in the grey dawn, as they looked around at the jumbled, whimpering mass of humanity cowering in tiny groups in every corner, were the results of the great fire really apparent.

Before morning, over two thousand native women and children had stormed their way into Fort William.

CHAPTER FIVE

50,000 against 500

Friday, June 18

One of the more fascinating aspects of the siege of Calcutta was the way in which the British consistently underrated the skill of the Nabob's forces. The bitter personal animosities among the leading personalities in the garrison were hardly conducive to coherent thinking, and without doubt contributed disastrously to the hazards menacing the settlement; but there was more to the situation than that. At no time had the British ever expected the Nabob's army to fight with discipline and intelligence. Nor had it probably occurred to Captain Minchin that Roy Doolub outstripped him as a highly astute commander. It seemed impossible. Roy Doolub was a heathen, the commander of an untrained rabble easily dispersed by a few well-directed cannon shots.

Unfortunately, however, this view was based on the only intelligence available; a jumbled series of reports of sporadic, punitive raids on small, undefended villages. One can imagine the British confidently prognosticating the Nabob's defeat over their Madeira. It was one thing to pursue a few unarmed civilians into the jungle. Let him wait until he came in contact with British guns and cold steel.

Yet the highly trained Bengali troops now locked in battle with the garrison had been fighting continuously

98

in a successful ten-year war against their formidable
Maratha neighbours. Nor was the undisciplined firing
and looting of the Bagh Bazaar their handiwork. The
sack of Black Town had been carried out by professional
plunderers—who were looked down upon with disdain
by the Nabob's crack troops who remained under strict
control throughout the battle.

This deep-rooted tendency to underrate the enemy
was partly responsible for the fatal lack of British planning, and consequently, on and after this crucial Friday,
the crumbling defensive plan degenerated into a series
of decisions made on the spur of the moment. Today
everything that happened on the first crucial day of the
siege takes on a strange nightmarish quality, and however many times one re-reads the original reports, one is
left wondering whether events could really have happened in the way they did. Time after time apparently
unaccountable decisions occur. The Moors would be
on the point of retreating, yet the British retired instead.
A battery that had never seen fighting would be evacuated,
but then the Moors would not bother to occupy it.

There was no overall plan and each local commander
did not seem to know or care what his subordinates, or
indeed anyone else, were doing. Though the battle was
fought over a very small area (roughly a rectangle little
more than a mile by half a mile), not one of the many
attacks seemed to bear the slightest relationship to one
another. A mansion would be occupied by the enemy,
who would be left there unmolested; while only a hundred yards away the British would hold out desperately
to prevent the enemy gaining another house which had
no apparent tactical value. All coherent plans (if ever
they truly existed) seemed to have vanished into the
powder-laden air which now hung like some horrible
deadening pall over the whole embattled area.

Looking back, one can see a dozen ways in which apparently forlorn situations might have been retrieved, occasions on which wasted lives might have been saved for the final stages of the siege. But having convinced themselves that their duty lay in remaining inside the Fort, Drake and Minchin isolated themselves there, so that the fate of the batteries and isolated pockets of men now depended on garbled reports of messengers. Consequently real control was lost, with the tragic but almost farcical result that reinforcements would be enthusiastically promised to a battery already retiring from its position, while simultaneously, orders to retreat would be sent to another at the very moment its confident garrison was poised to launch a successful attack.

The crucial point of Friday's attack was the east battery, where Holwell was second-in-command to Captain Clayton. The junior officers included the brilliant French gunner, Lieutenant Lebeaume, 'who had left Chandernagore on a point of honour', and Ensign Carstairs; these two made a magnificent stand despite heavy losses and there is no doubt that had the battery been commanded by a more energetic and resourceful officer, it could have held out much longer than it did. Holwell tried his best, but as we shall see, he was powerless to influence Clayton.

The battery stood at the corner of The Avenue and Rope Walk. It had no roof, but its wooden palisades were solid and the breastwork, several feet thick, consisted of earth thrown up from the wide trench which had been dug in front of it. It was shielded on the right by the Park wall, on the left by the wall of the compound surrounding the Court-house. Sandbags lined the inside of what was in effect a three-sided walled enclosure, open at the back, from which the troops could plainly see the Fort a quarter of a mile away. In front of the battery The Avenue continued for five hundred yards to the cross-roads which marked the eastern extremity of White Town.

Clearly visible to the garrison was the gaol, the last building in White Town, situated at the cross-roads, and it was here, after much argument, that Lebeaume made his first stand. He argued that by occupying the gaol he would prevent the enemy seizing the houses on Rope Walk which flanked the battery. Clayton hesitated. He was a short, irritable man with a passion for shooting and fishing and based his objections on the grounds that it would weaken his battery, but he finally agreed; only, one feels, because he was weary of Lebeaume's arguments.

During the night, Lebeaume with two cannon, seventeen trained men and forty Indian musketeers crept out to the gaol and spent the hours before dawn breaking holes in the thin walls for the cannon and muskets. No coolies were left, but four times during the night Lebeaume led parties back to the battery to carry up powder, grape and cannon-balls which he stocked in the gaol's single bare room, about thirty feet by twenty; or in the compound, near a stagnant well with its precious water for cooling the cannon.

He had conceived a daring plan, and before first light placed his two six-pounders in the roadway in front of the gaol with the idea of surprising the enemy. (He prudently neglected to inform his superior officer in case his plan was vetoed.) By daybreak, his small force was ready at the cross-roads, on the other side of which five thousand Indian troops were awaiting the order to attack.

Lebeaume was by all accounts a silent, introspective man who must sometimes have felt a little lost; he was an alien among the British and news of the fighting in Europe between the two countries probably divided his loyalties. Apart from issuing necessary orders, he rarely spoke during the nine hours his battery held out. He waited in silence now as the little garrison became aware that the Indians were about to attack. They could hear the shuffle of feet, the clank of arms; and then the steady tramping as the first wave, some four hundred strong, marched with parade-ground discipline to the point where they would commence their charge. Lebeaume waited no longer; opening fire at point-blank range, he showered the astonished Indians with red-hot grape, and in an instant the orderly ranks were plunged into bloodstained confusion.

Almost before the smoke from Lebeaume's guns had cleared, however, St Jacques opened a long-range plunging fire. His third shot tore through the gaol walls, killing three, and now a full-scale assault was launched on the gaol.

In the early stages it was the story of Perrin's Redoubt all over again. Incessant Indian attacks in great strength were flung back with heavy losses. But now there came a moment when Lebeaume could no longer hold his position in the open road (due largely to the time which it took to load his guns), and by nine o'clock, after severe hand-to-hand fighting, he managed to drag his cannon back to the gaol which, during the action, had received three more direct hits.

Here in this outpost some five hundred yards in front of the battery, he held out for hours against vast odds in a fashion which now seems almost miraculous. He had only himself and fifty-seven men. He was pitted against a minimum of five thousand Indians. He was not only outnumbered, he was outgunned. More than once the enemy actually reached the gaol and were only driven off by desperate hand-to-hand fighting. It seemed as though sheer weight would force an entry—that after the

first, then the second, then the third Indian had been
killed, the fourth, stepping into their places, would be
one too many. The battle raged in blinding sunshine
and deadly heat, for the temperature was over a hundred.
And yet Lebeaume, with twenty-five of his men dead
around him, managed to hold the gaol until three o'clock.

At the cross-roads, dawn had brought a violence that
bred courage. In Fort William, it ushered in confusion
that bred despair and led to paralysing irresolution.

Friday was a beautiful, if hot, morning with the mist
hanging like a blanket low over the Hoogly, and soon
after dawn Peter and Mary Carey were leaning on the
west parapet when they were joined by Lieutenant Blagg.
Blagg was only twenty-one and one has the impression
of an intelligent youngster, more sensitive than the usual
run of merchants or soldiers in Bengal. In fact, Blagg
would have fitted much better into the India of a century
later.

Below them, knee-deep in the river, scantily clad men
and women were washing, swilling the dirty brown
water over their heads. So normal and peaceful was the
scene, so complete the bathers' preoccupation with their
daily ritual, that the watchers for a moment were content
with the illusion that this could be the beginning of a
day that had never known siege; a peaceful day with
its familiar, easygoing routine of work, followed by a
good curry lunch, archery or rowing in the afternoon, a
walk in The Park, some arrack and a hookah after dinner.
Everything appeared quiet, as though the few great
houses they could see on the river bank were not yet
awake (in fact they were empty), and on the opposite
bank of the Hoogly thin trails of smoke were rising from
the first fires in the scattered villages.

As they turned away from the river, however, the reality of their situation was distressingly and suddenly apparent. It was almost impossible to move as all around them those on the parade-ground woke to a new day. Over two thousand ragged refugees, clutching their few possessions, huddled on the open ground between the Governor's House and the arcade. As Blagg tried to cross to the south-east bastion, he had to fight his way through a solid mass of cowering, frightened, tired human beings packed so tightly in places that it was impossible to walk between them. All order had vanished and the parade-ground, which for years had been brushed each morning as carefully as the Governor's broadcloth coat, had become in one night a dirty square in which the private lives of men, women and children were displayed in public without embarrassment, only with a sullen anger. All the filth, the flies, the germs and, above all, the stench of the bazaar had come right into Fort William itself at the one vital moment when it should have been stripped for action.

The plight of the Englishwomen and their babies was little better, even though they struggled to maintain the elementary rules of hygiene. The evening before, the children had been taken back to their mothers in Writers' Row, but within an hour of dawn the heat was beating down, creeping through the latticed air-holes. There was no comfort. Bedding had been taken away to prepare for the wounded. Elizabeth Dumbleton, the notary's wife, spent the night with her one dress folded up as a pillow, and used her two cotton petticoats to cover her children, aged two and four, against the flies. Anne Mackett, awaiting the birth of her child, had salvaged a little straw from the company stables. A soldier had carried in some more for Sarah Mapletoft and her two babies.

The thirsty children seldom stopped whimpering, and although Mary Carey tried to keep a fire going at the end of the corridor in order to boil water, the outbreak of violent diarrhoea was steadily increasing. There were no medicines available. The rooms in Writers' Row were in one long line with a passage running the full length. It must have looked rather like the interior of a corridor train—with every so often a room being used as a latrine. But these primitive lavatories were wholly inadequate, and as no attempt had been made to build them away from the living quarters, some unlucky mothers were next door to these makeshift privies, which were only emptied on the rare occasions when a soldier could be spared for an hour to dump the contents in the Hoogly.

The diarrhoea was bad enough, but the flies were probably worse. (Lady Russell in normal times had four servants whose sole occupation was the wielding of fly-whisks.) The flies settled in their thousands on the privies. The women tried to brush them away from their babies, but it was impossible; indeed, the flies were more frightening than the enemy, for they crawled round the eyes, in the mouths and ears and up the nostrils of each child. And, as though the flies and mosquitoes were not enough, another insect now appeared: 'above all the bug-fly is disgusting—one of them will scent a room; they are in form like a ladybird but their smell is a thousand times more offensive.'

It is not difficult to imagine the dismay which the civilians' plight must have instilled in Drake and his senior officers. But at no time do they seem to have taken any steps to lighten their suffering. Indeed here, as with the more pressing military problems, they merely wasted most of the morning in fruitless argument.

If they did discuss the military situation, they must

at first have found it promising. The feint attack on the north battery had been repulsed. The south battery had hardly fired a shot. The gaol was holding out splendidly, and the few cannon shots aimed at the Fort had screeched over harmlessly. But this favourable situation does not seem to have spurred Drake into any semblance of aggressive action, and when the commanders met in the council chamber at nine a.m., there is no record that they discussed any plans for exploiting the situation and pushing home their first successes. Instead, they wrangled incessantly.

It was the garrison's one chance for an effective counter-attack. Yet nothing was done and a hundred questions spring to mind. What had happened to the eighteen-pounder so effectively used at Perrin's by Lieutenant Blagg? Could it not have been dragged into The Park and fired over the battery and gaol into the Indian positions? Could the troops who had repulsed the attack on the north battery not have been sent out to harry the retreating Indians? Or, better still, could they not have moved up through Black Town (outside the so-called defence line) and opened up an attack on the Moors' northern flank, with perhaps Blagg or Piccard crossing The Park, passing Lady Russell's house and simultaneously attacking the Indians from the south? From this distance it all seems so simple. The men were available, the Fort was in no immediate danger, and the battle at Perrin's had shown with startling clarity how the Indians became demoralized when a determined British attack took their assaulting masses in flank. Yet nothing was done. The senior officers were too busy squabbling interminably over problems which a strong Governor could have—should have—decided on the spot.

Manningham wanted the immediate evacuation of all

women and children. Minchin claimed this was impracticable in daylight. Drake was incapable of making
any decision, even the wrong one, and the arguments
went on interminably. Minchin was anxious that the
two thousand refugees be turned out of the Fort. Manningham felt it would cause rioting and the militia would
refuse to fight. Frankland wanted the Fort completely
evacuated, but Minchin believed that the Nabob was
still bluffing and would never attack the Fort directly.
(In the midst of these deliberations, the Reverend Mapletoft temporarily left his post to see how his pregnant
wife was faring, and, being unable to find her, burst
into the council chamber demanding an immediate
search!) Grant at least tried to get some estimate of the
powder reserves, but when Minchin sent for Witherington he could not be found for half an hour.

Next, a message was received from the east battery.
Drake, expecting vital information, told the sentry to
admit the messenger immediately. His message *was*
important—the men had not eaten for twelve hours—
and only now did it become apparent that nobody had
arranged to provide food for the garrisons of the outposts. But when Drake belatedly ordered rations to be
sent to these hungry men, it was discovered that although
the Fort had plenty of rice and wheat to withstand a long
siege, not a single pot or pan had been requisitioned so
that now it could not be cooked. Only dry biscuits
reached the outposts that day.

As one studies the reports, these futile, bickering men
remind one of the all-too-familiar committees which
nowadays meet leisurely to formulate long-term plans
for saving some starving tribe but in this process become
so occupied with agendas and sub-committees that the
tribe becomes extinct before a satisfactory plan is
reached. When one pictures Drake and his companions

in the council chamber, quarrelling in the heat, doing nothing, it is sometimes difficult to remember that less than half a mile away Lebeaume and his men were fighting for their lives.

The Frenchman was still holding out, but against onslaughts now becoming so ferocious that by eleven o'clock Clayton and Holwell in the battery five hundred yards behind were left with no illusion as to the terrible punishment the garrison of the gaol was taking. Holwell volunteered to gallop over to them and suggest that Lebeaume retreat to the battery.

Arriving flushed and panting from his hazardous dash, he was appalled at what he saw. There had been no time to bury the dead. Musket-fire was now unceasing, and, peering through a loophole, he could see some Indians beginning to infiltrate southwards behind the gaol towards Rope Walk. But when he suggested that Lebeaume should retire and offered to send a relief party to cover him, the Frenchman refused. His decision showed remarkable spirit, especially since he was convinced his chances of holding out were slim unless Clayton, back in the battery, could be persuaded to send out a raiding party to infiltrate behind the northern flank of the enemy.

Lebeaume's plan was sound, but on returning to the battery, Holwell discovered that Clayton refused absolutely to commit any men to a flanking move. Desperately Holwell begged his commander to realize that the battery was in no immediate danger (and wouldn't be so long as Lebeaume held the gaol), but Clayton had a fixation about weakening the battery's garrison. In the end, he reluctantly agreed to send Ensign Carstairs and twenty men to reinforce Lebeaume, but made it clear that on no account was Carstairs to leave the gaol unless it was to retreat.

There was nothing more Holwell could do, though,

as he wrote later, 'there was no impediment that could have obstructed the detachment arriving directly close on the back of the enemy, who would have been between two fires, without hardly a possibility of a tithe of the whole body escaping a repulse and slaughter which, I am convinced, would have struck such a panic in the enemy as . . . had obliged the Nabob to have . . . dropped his designs against us.'

This may have been too sanguine an appraisal, but a glorious opportunity for offensive action was lost, for Carstairs had hardly settled his men in the gaol before the Indians seized their first house on Rope Walk and started moving westwards to the more crowded dwellings south of The Park. Suddenly the Nabob's colours flew from the roof of Lady Russell's mansion.

From now on the men in the battery could not always see the Indians moving to the attack behind compound walls, and became aware of a fresh house having fallen only through the Indians' habit of announcing each victory by hoisting flags.

On this occasion Clayton acted energetically, and with uncharacteristic zeal, trained his eighteen-pounder on the house, and blew off most of the first storey, starting a fire. The Indians bolted, but a few minutes later reinforcements were rushed up, the fire was put out and their flag was once more in evidence on the rooftop.

Flushed with success, they pressed on among the houses until very soon they had captured Dumbleton's, which stood less than a hundred yards from the battery. From its rooftop they were now able to fire down on the roofless east battery so that Clayton's men could only move close to the walls. The fire from this quarter was 'so exceeding hot' that Clayton sent a messenger back to Drake, who ordered John Bellamy and ten men to move across The Park. Covered by cannon-fire from the battery, they drove the enemy out of Dumbleton's house, but despite this setback, other Indian forces moved under cover of Lady Russell's walls to the houses south of The Park; here they were sheltered by dozens of alleys between the walls of each compound. They did not attack the south battery directly (except for the occasional fire-arrow), but seemed content to occupy more houses, signalling each new victory by hoisting more flags which could be clearly seen in the Fort. Cannon-fire dislodged some of the enemy, but it was dangerous to pick out targets as British troops still occupied some houses. This is possibly why the south battery made no attempt to check the infiltration; their line of fire was also blocked by several houses, including Clayton's, Grant's and Witherington's.

By mid-morning, many of the largest houses were in enemy hands, but the pattern of occupation was chaotic. The Nabob's troops in Lady Russell's house, for example, kept peppering the east battery; yet next door John Bellamy was still firmly established in Dumbleton's house. Neither seemed inclined to attack the other. Indeed, the sporadic occupation of houses had an unreal, dreamlike quality, especially among the coloured fighters on both sides. In some strange way the instincts of people who did not really hate each other told them not to attack unless provoked. They were enemies, of course, and eventually one side had to win, but they were like litigants unwillingly forced into a complicated lawsuit, who, when they sit in the same court-room, become uncomfortably aware that their opponent is not such a bad fellow after all.

There was of course a very real danger in the events now developing. Immediately, it seemed to lie in the possibility of those Indians who had got south of The Park moving northwards across its open space to cut off the east battery. Drake, however, never realized this. As we shall see, he was obstinately preoccupied with the quite irrelevant prospect of danger to the south battery. So throughout the morning the struggle for the houses continued in this bizarre manner, with the Moors cheering as they reached one house, the British cheering as they became their next-door neighbours. Yet this was no comic-opera engagement, but a deadly prelude to what was about to follow. The British, from the tops and windows of the houses, kept a constant fire on the enemy as they advanced under cover of the neighbouring houses, but they were so outnumbered that it was impossible to hold on to every house. When the fire became too hot, the British party would retreat, though on at least one occasion the small garrison was trapped.

This happened to Lieutenant Blagg who had been sent to hold Minchin's house, a mansion of considerable tactical value. Blagg's stand here—in which he lost two men, but killed one hundred and seventy-three Indians —was in its own way as heroic as Lebeaume's defence of the gaol, and in order to appreciate his ordeal it becomes necessary to describe the house and grounds in which the commander lived in a style that would have astounded any officer of equivalent rank in England.

Minchin's ostentatious mansion followed the usual Calcutta pattern, with the living and sleeping quarters situated on the first floor in the hope of capturing the occasional breeze. Broad stairs swept up from an enormous front hall that would have accommodated a hundred people (but was never used). Behind the hall, a smaller servants' stairway led to the same landing. Like every house belonging to a senior member of the Company, it was nearly a hundred feet long and surrounded by a balcony.

Minchin's living-room and study, fifty feet long, was

crammed with furniture he had accumulated over the
years; teak or ebony armchairs, glass shades, brass
lamps, indifferent pictures, clocks, card tables, four Japan
stands, and a big desk that was almost lost in one corner.

In the walled compound, which had a main gate and
a smaller one at the rear, one building contained kitchens
and a bakery, another living quarters for Minchin's
twenty or so servants and gardeners, who kept poultry-
runs and grew every vegetable from cucumbers and
lettuce to guavas, mangoes and that strange new fruit,
the pomegranate. At the bottom of his garden his stables,
built of solid posts with a palm-thatched roof, were large
enough for a dozen horses and four carriages.

After a rapid reconnaissance, Lieutenant Blagg decided
to try and hold the ground floor for as long as possible,
only withdrawing to the landing if the position became
untenable. A display of strength was vital to overawe
the enemy, so he sent relays of men in turn to man the
roof and windows whence they could fire at any Indian
unwise enough to venture too close, while the main
garrison remained grouped round or under the foot of
the main staircase which provided some cover. Despite
the fire from the roof, the Indians made several attempts
to force the heavy main door (which had been specially
built to resist dacoits), but these were beaten back without
loss and the few enemy who appeared at the windows
were either driven off or shot.

Blagg's hope of fighting on the ground floor was based
on the knowledge that two other near-by houses—
Putham's and Grant's—were firmly held by the British,
and that the Moors were so busy occupying other houses
elsewhere that they had little time or inclination to launch
full-scale attacks on those in British hands. Suddenly,
however, the entire situation changed. We do not know
quite what happened, nor the exact time. Peter Carey

was firing from the roof when he saw something that made him stumble down the stairs to find Blagg as quickly as he could. The Nabob's colours were being hoisted on the roofs of Putham's and Grant's houses.

Within minutes the Moors were swarming across the compound of Minchin's house, grouping themselves for an attack in the shelter of the cook-house not fifty yards away, and Blagg was already in a hopeless position. From the moment the enemy had occupied the neighbouring houses, Blagg had become trapped.

The cause of this disaster seems to have been Drake's obsession with the south battery. Convinced it was about to be cut off, he had almost decided to order its garrison to retreat. First, however, he must have felt it prudent to evacuate the few men in the houses south of The Park. We do not know who occupied the two houses adjacent to Blagg so we have no record that they actually received such orders; but the fact that the Moors entered without opposition indicates an orderly withdrawal. Possibly a similar message to Blagg may have gone astray. (The terrain was admirably suited to sniping, and scores of Portuguese and Armenian troops who were sent on missions were never seen again, a percentage of them probably deserting.)

Blagg's position was now desperate. For nearly an hour he managed to keep the enemy out of the front hall, but when the groaning hinges of the big door indicated that it was on the point of giving way, he was forced to retreat to the first landing. All Minchin's furniture was taken from the rooms to form a barricade. Heavy chests, tables and beds were placed by the top of the stairway with anything else that could be found. Mattresses were placed between the furniture.

Though the barricade was hardly finished before the enemy burst the front door open, it was, for the time being, serviceable enough, and though trapped, Blagg's muskets commanded both staircases; neither was likely to be rushed successfully by the enemy. What worried Blagg much more acutely was his rapidly dwindling powder supply.

While Blagg was facing disaster, less than half a mile away in the Fort Lady Russell had tried to see the Governor several times that morning. Soon after dawn she and Anna Bellamy and Mary Carey had taken the children back to the arcade, but the heat was so stifling there that she decided it would soon overcome her small charges. The stench of the refugees huddled directly in front of them, their cries and moans, their insanitary habits, the flies, the crowded little room, above all the insufferable heat—if this went on some of the children must collapse. The incessant cries of the babies drowned Janniko's music even though he fiddled as he had never fiddled before.

Lady Russell cornered Drake in the council chamber and demanded better accommodation for the children. It must have been a trying moment for the harassed Governor, suddenly confronted by a woman whose temper was as short as her stature. The embarrassed Drake told her there was no more room. But Lady Russell knew better. What about the Governor's ballroom on the first floor? Drake must have been horrified. But Lady Russell gained her point and he agreed that the ballroom could be turned into a nursery.

Lady Russell immediately set about preparing to move the children. Mary had the idea of telling them they were going to play a variation of follow-my-leader. Janniko would lead the way; they were to follow him. Lady Russell promised a prize for the best-behaved child.

A few minutes later a winding procession emerged from the darkness of the arcade, following Janniko as he pranced ahead, his tiny dwarf-like body almost dancing as he fiddled away, twisting and turning across the crowded parade-ground, forcing a path between the refugees, while Anna, Mary and Lady Russell carried those too tiny to walk. The procession was half-way to the Governor's House when, over a thousand yards away, St Jacques opened fire with his eighteen-pounder.

Small faces must have looked up, terrified at the boom of the gun which had already scored two direct—but ineffectual—hits on the Fort. 'Down, everybody!' some-one must have shrieked, but Janniko was some way ahead and apparently did not hear. The ball landed in the heart of the refugees, not six feet from the fiddler. He appeared to spin round, as his music slithered down in a waterfall of sound. Poor Janniko probably never knew what killed him.

The children—some distance behind the fiddler—had a miraculous escape, but in one moment the parade-ground around them was a tangle of dead and living, of screams as the raw surface of humanity emerged and the nerves of the living snapped in rage, fear and misery.

Lady Russell and the others scrambled up, gathered the children and tried to divert their attention from what was happening around them, but one doubts whether they ever succeeded, for men and women started fighting as they lay injured, screaming abuse at the British and Nabob alike. One old woman took up a pannikin of water to drink, then hurled it away with a curse and the liquid splashed red over the dress of Dumbleton's baby daughter. It was not water but the blood from a dying man.

Amid piteous wails of misery from the Indians, this remarkable woman managed to get the children off the parade-ground before three European soldiers came to cart away the dead.

Sarah Mapletoft's baby was born that day. Dorothy Bellamy was in her own room when she heard Sarah's thin wail (though she had been wailing regularly for some time); but when she went in, she knew immediately that this time the baby was ready to be born. The room was next to one of the latrines, but it was the largest in Writers' Row. Sarah Mapletoft lay on a small cot covered with straw, and no longer had the strength or inclination to complain about her life in Calcutta.

The room was stifling. The stench was abominable. And Dorothy was alone and sixty. She managed to find the large pan in which Mary had been boiling water, and ran down to the Hoogly to fill it since this was now the only water available. When she returned, Sarah was groaning. Dorothy picked up her dirty old towel and tied it to the head of the cot so that Sarah could grip it and pull when the pains were at their worst. Then she pulled off Sarah's underskirt and folded it between her legs; next she took off her own underskirt and put this makeshift sheet between Sarah's body and the straw.

Dorothy had no medicines, no surgical instruments, and nobody in the Fort had the faintest idea where Surgeon Gray could be found. She could do nothing but try to make Sarah comfortable, moisten her dry, cracked lips with water, and above all wave away the scores of flies that kept settling and crawling over Sarah's face and body.

An hour and a half later the baby was born, the only one during the siege. It was a fine girl, later christened Constantia.

Many historians have attempted to analyse the reasons

which made Drake panic at a moment when the balance
between victory and defeat may well have been separated
by no more than a hairsbreadth. It is true that Drake did
not know this, but he must certainly have been aware that
his men were fighting magnificently; and yet suddenly,
unaccountably, after hours of irresolution, he seems to
have been stimulated to action. And panic.

No doubt his unpopularity weighed heavily on him.
He was a lonely, bitter and frustrated man, and it is much
easier to fight a desperate campaign when surrounded by
friends and advisers (however tiresome the latter may
be). Moreover, one is apt to forget that in 1756 Calcutta
might as well have been on the moon for all the contact
it had with the rest of the world. London was a year
away; even Madras was another world.

At the best of times a sense of loneliness and responsibility accentuates the normal apprehensions of a commander; but at least his loneliness can be interrupted
by the arrival of newcomers, the need for reports, the
signals from headquarters. In Calcutta, no such support
was available. The leaders of the settlement were on
their own. Leadenhall Street, which appointed them,
paid their salaries, organized their shipping, encouraged
their fortunes—Leadenhall Street hadn't even the faintest
idea what was happening; and would never know until
they were all dead. This realization that authority had
no conception of their plight must have tormented Drake.
Even the Christians in the Roman arenas derived strength
from the spectators. But Drake—and many others—
lacked that magical stimulus to courage. They had no
spectators. They were alone. Worse. Nobody knew.
Probably nobody cared.

But perhaps more than anything else, his decisions
may have been swayed by the ever-present sight of the
refugees in the Fort. Not for a moment could he escape

them; their wavering panic; the dirt and flies they had brought on to his beloved parade-ground; their moans and pleas for food, interrupted only by the high whistle of cannon-balls whining over the Fort. And as though these things were not enough, he was bedevilled by Manningham's pestering demands or Minchin's insolent silence.

In his fuddled mood the panic around him must have created an illusion of hopeless defeat. The Fort had never seriously been threatened, yet it presented a picture that dismayed and frightened him. It struck him as being on the verge of defeat, and before long this impression began to include the whole of White Town and even extended to the batteries, of whose activities he was in total ignorance.

For at this time—around four o'clock—there was not the slightest cause for panic. The east battery, despite heavy casualties, had withstood every attack; the south battery was virtually unmolested. The men of the north battery had hardly fired a shot since the first modest attack at dawn. Blagg was still holding out. In fact, all along the scattered perimeter the British were holding their own against enormous odds, and were inflicting appalling losses. If they could only hold until nightfall, the whole position might change for the better. And yet, within an hour, the garrison was overtaken by disaster.

At three o'clock Lebeaume had been forced to retreat from the gaol. It was a setback, but it was neither fatal nor unexpected. His stand had prevented the Moors from launching an all-out attack on the east battery, which should now have been ready to withstand all onslaughts until dark. Both Lebeaume and Carstairs were wounded, but they managed to drag their cannon back to the east battery, leaving twenty-five dead behind. The Moors immediately seized the gaol and St Jacques lost no time in bringing up his heavy guns. Even so, the east battery was capable of demolishing the gaol more easily than St Jacques could demolish the battery. Despite this, two men panicked—Drake and Clayton.

For some reason which he never later explained, Drake's phobia that the south battery was in danger increased, so that apparently he gave little thought to the east battery which was in a much more serious position. There seems no logical explanation. Perhaps the Moorish flags flying on the houses south of The Park frightened Drake. There were more houses than on Rope Walk, so presumably there were more enemy flags. One cannot look for reasons. Drake was convinced of a danger that did not exist, and suddenly, between four and five o'clock, without any prior discussion, he ordered Captain Buchanan to withdraw to a reserve south battery half-way along the south road between the battery proper and the Fort. This reserve battery was little more than a single palisade with earthworks.

It was an incredible decision, for though Buchanan's men had not been involved in serious fighting, the very presence of their guns had effectively stopped the enemy from occupying many houses lying opposite the hospital. After he had retired the Moors did not bother for some time to occupy the deserted battery, but immediately entered all the houses facing directly on to the south road.

At roughly the same time, Captain Clayton announced that he wanted to retreat from the east battery with all speed. Holwell and Lebeaume were horrified, for though the battery had been under constant attack, both were convinced it could be held until dusk.

There was apparently a stormy scene, not difficult to imagine, as Lebeaume, crouching behind the palisade to escape the musket-fire all around them, accused Clayton of cowardice and offered to hold the battery under Holwell if Clayton cared to leave alone. It was not a scene calculated to imbue the tired troops with new zest, but this open accusation did at least have one good effect. After some argument, Clayton gave his word that he would fight on while Holwell went to ask Drake for permission to retire or for reinforcements. The promise was given on the understanding that Holwell and Lebeaume would agree to retreat if the Governor ordered it.

Holwell galloped back to the Fort and saw Drake immediately. Fortunately Grant was present, for at first the Governor said in effect that if Clayton wanted to retreat, that was his affair. Grant, however, begged him to send reinforcements, 'knowing how fatal this [retreat] would be'. It was imperative, he insisted, that the east battery should be held until the following day in view of a possible evacuation. If the battery went, the Moors would be at the gates of the fort and infiltrate round to the river bank, where the guns were useless. This, more than anything else, must have made Drake change his mind, for the thought of having his line of retreat cut terrified him. He finally agreed to send out seventy fresh troops and two eighteen-pounders.

There was no time to lose. Holwell asked Grant to ride back with him and tell Clayton the good news, and the two men, filled with new hope, galloped off together along The Avenue.

They had almost reached the Court-house when they were confronted by a scene that made them rein in their horses in stupefaction. At the very moment when reinforcements were on their way, a bedraggled procession was staggering towards them. The east battery was in full, disorderly retreat.

Grant dashed forward to demand an explanation. The battery, mumbled Clayton, had lost another ten men. It was impossible to fight on any longer. One can picture these two men, standing there arguing, the resigned troops resting on the roadway, Grant crying that seventy fresh troops were virtually on their way.

Grant begged the men to return 'but when I ordered half the men to lay down their arms in order to draw first the eighteen-pounder while the other half stood with their arms for defence of the battery, not a man would stir or pull a rope'. Holwell too tried to rouse the men and seized the rope of one of the field-pieces, hoping they would follow his example; but nobody moved. Where, he asked, were the heavier cannon? Spiked, said a sergeant. Where was Lebeaume? Where was Carstairs? Evacuated with the other wounded while Holwell had been arguing with Drake. Half a dozen soldiers waited no longer, but started trudging towards the Fort.

There was nothing anybody could do now; argument and recrimination were pointless. Holwell stood hatless in the burning sun and looked past the file of men trudging along The Avenue up which he had walked in peace with old Bellamy so many evenings of his life. There was debris everywhere in the shimmering heat. Houses which he had visited only a few days previously were already charred shells. Through compound walls shattered by cannon-fire, he could catch glimpses of a picnic table still standing under the bower that Anne Mackett had planted; a pair of saddles on the ground mildewed through neglect; a forgotten pony, still tied to a post, whinnying.

Holwell's thoughts must have been bitter, but how much blacker would have been his despair and frustration had he known that at the very moment when he had been pleading with Drake, Roy Doolub was considering withdrawing *his* troops. For hours the Indian general had watched his men launch themselves fruitlessly against the gaol and then the battery itself. He had never wanted to attack in this manner. The losses had again been appalling, and Roy Doolub believed his tired men to be on the verge of panic. So, incredibly, almost at the same time that Clayton was withdrawing, thousands of Indians were on the verge of retiring.

Neither Roy Doolub nor Clayton realized the bizarre, ironic twist which the battle had suddenly taken, as though two groups of people had suddenly decided simultaneously to turn their backs on each other. Neither of the commanders had the faintest suspicion of what the other was doing.

The Indians who had captured the gaol were the first to realize what had happened, for they could now actually see Clayton's men stumbling along The Avenue and were quick to move in and occupy the east battery. Those watching from the Fort did not of course know Roy Doolub's plans, but they too could see Clayton's men and Drake had news of the retreat from sentries on the east curtain before Holwell and Grant could ride back.

As soon as he realized what had happened, Drake immediately ordered Captain Smith to evacuate the north battery, then told Buchanan (who had barely installed himself in the reserve battery) to abandon it and return to the Fort. By the time the exhausted and frustrated Holwell entered the council chamber, the Governor was ready to announce a new plan of defence.

Captain Clayton would take half his men and hold the church. The other half would go to Mr Eyre's house which commanded the north-east bastion. Men from the north battery would go to Cruttenden's house, north of the Fort. Thirty men from the south battery would occupy the Company's house to the south. By doing this, Drake hoped to establish a shorter defence-line in houses that commanded the Fort. It almost exactly matched the same compromise plan Holwell himself had suggested before the siege began. Only now it was far too late, and 'the position now was this: instead of having terrified the Nawab [Nabob] by the vigour of their resistance, the British had been beaten back in a few hours' fighting from a line which they had hoped to be able to defend for some days.'

The meeting was about to break up when someone asked about Lieutenant Blagg. Everybody had forgotten Blagg and his men. Drake blustered that they would get a relief party through somehow, whereupon Grant said it was impossible, the Indians were already swarming across The Park.

It was finally agreed that Henry Lushington should take a field-piece and twenty men to the south-west corner of The Park in the hope of helping Blagg with supporting fire should he ever be able to break out of Minchin's house.

For four hours now the ten weary men had been holding out on the landing of Minchin's house. Time after time the Indians had fought their way to the top of the stairs, on each occasion being beaten back at point-blank range. It was only when the Indians began to use fire-arrows that Blagg was forced to take refuge on the roof.

The first arrow, dipped in boiling oil, then set alight, sank straight into a mattress in the barricade. As the straw burst into flames, scores of Indians surged through the hall door. Blagg waited until they crowded the stairs, hardly visible in the smoke, then he and Smith hurled the burning mattress over the top of the banister rails. As the screaming men fell over one another, the ten defenders scrambled up the small ladder and through the roof trapdoor. But Blagg knew it was only a respite;

they were now down to three musket- or pistol-shots each.

Now came a series of attacks which for an hour the little garrison managed to fight off with swords or cutlasses when the Indians attempted to scale the walls with bamboo ladders. Despite their resolution, however, Blagg was soon forced to tell his men that they faced two alternatives: either to stay and be killed, or try to fight their way out with their swords. There was, in fact, no real choice.

Eight of the garrison were Company servants or sailors, and in a cool, calm manner Blagg planned the final rush. They were down to one shot each. Carey was to open the trap and then five men would empty their muskets or pistols into the Indians on the landing, taking them by surprise. Immediately this had been done the remaining five were also to fire their last shots. Then all of them would jump down on to the landing and fight their way past the Indians on the stairs amid the confusion. After that only one thing mattered. They must stick together or each would be fighting ten men. Blagg and Carey would be in front, Smith and Wilkinson would bring up the rear.

The waiting must have been intolerable, for they had no food or water, no shade on the roof from the pitiless sun, so that half the men lay gasping and heaving like newly-landed fish. But perhaps worst of all was the stench of the corpses. Nothing—not the stairs, not the roof ladder, not the trapdoor—could stifle it. Five hours is a long time in a tropical country, and Indian bodies by the score had been left not only in the compound but in the hall, where at least fifty had been killed. The suffocating smell penetrated everywhere.

When the moment came, Blagg led them in a wild rush down the stairs. Once the last precious ten shots had been fired, the small knot of men cut their way towards the door. The swords rose and fell and the momentum was so great that those who were wounded hardly noticed the ripping of clothing, the pain or the blood. The little party had almost reached the front gate before it seemed to slow down. The men were tiring and no one knows just how they started to separate. They were close to the compound gate when Blagg heard the sound of a cannon and one of his men shouted out to him that a relief party was waiting outside the heavy gate. In their excitement they must have forgotten his orders to stay close together. Bob Wilkinson was the first to be cut off. According to the records, he was attacked by four men at once, but cut down three before, badly wounded in one shoulder, he threw down his sword and asked for quarter. The Moors, either inflamed by their losses or not realizing what he was doing, hacked him to pieces as he fell.

Charlie Smith had also become isolated and now they turned on him; but then a curious thing happened. The Moors strictly obeyed the formal rules of war, and an officer, apparently horrified that Wilkinson had been refused quarter, stopped the fighting around Smith. It was an almost impossible moment. Barely a few yards away Blagg and the others were fighting their way to the gate. At Smith's feet lay Wilkinson's dead body. Yet in the tiny oasis around the isolated Smith, the fighting ceased as the Nabob's officer offered him quarter.

Smith, we have it, yelled defiance and refused to accept. The Moors' idea of honour was thus satisfied and he was instantly attacked. He killed two men before being submerged under a wave of brown bodies. He vanished almost at the same moment as the other eight reached the gate and saw the welcome faces of Lushington's relief party.

Smith and Wilkinson were the only two casualties in the siege of Minchin's house, in which ten men had held out for five hours and killed at least one hundred and seventy-three Indians, a figure later admitted by the Nabob. Both were apprentices from Writers' Row. Charlie Smith was twenty-three. Bob Wilkinson was twenty.

CHAPTER SIX

The Women who stayed behind

Friday, June 18, dusk—Saturday, June 19, dawn

The women and children were evacuated that night once Drake had finally agreed that Manningham and Frankland were to supervise the operation. Although there was little danger of the enemy interfering, since it was unlikely they had any inkling of what was happening, the evacuation was none the less carried out in ghostlike silence and secrecy because of the very real danger of the refugees panicking. The poor wretches could see from their cramped quarters nearly twenty vessels anchored in the Hoogly. Were they even to begin to suspect that European women and children were being evacuated and abandoning them to their fate, it was easy to foresee the stampede which would ensue in a mad rush to gain the vessels with their bobbing lanterns offering apparent security.

The evacuation was to be carried out in two parts and through two different gates. The children, who were still in Drake's ballroom, would be taken through the colonnade leading directly to the Governor's private *ghat*, or wharf. John Bellamy, Henry Lushington and ten soldiers were detailed to guard them. Lady Russell, Anna and Mary would take them across in three batches and remain on the vessel with them. The other women would board the budgerows at the back gate below the flagpole in the northern section of the Fort. The wives could reach it directly from Writers' Row without being seen, providing the guard at the passage between the north and south sections of the Fort prevented any refugees leaving the parade-ground. Gervas Bellamy and his eldest son Thomas were detailed to shepherd the women to the boats.

The choice of Manningham and Frankland to supervise the evacuation was to have disastrous consequences, for no sooner had this unscrupulous couple been appointed than they decided the women and children should be taken to the *Dodaldy* (of which they were conveniently part-owners). Manningham posted himself at the Governor's gate, Frankland at the back gate. There can be little doubt that even before the women left the Fort, they had planned to remain on board with them if they could manufacture a suitable excuse.

No historian can tell us just how many children lived through the siege, but a study of the registers of Calcutta births and deaths indicates that there were probably between thirty and forty, and by eight o'clock these small creatures were ready to be embarked. Anna was to take the first boatload, which included the two Dumbleton children; Mary Carey the second; Lady Russell the last.

It must have been a ghostlike scene as the sleepy, wondering children were awakened, warned to be silent, and assembled into groups in the dimly-lit 'nursery'. Only promises that they would soon be reunited on board had succeeded in preventing their mothers from joining them, but many of the babies cried unceasingly and could not understand the reason for disturbing them. There seems to have been sporadic gunfire, so that even when Anna quieted the babies, each new flash would frighten them again.

Anna went first, and she had no serious trouble. Once her sleepy group was assembled, she led it through the colonnade to the Governor's gate where a budgerow with two sailors was waiting. Behind them fire-arrows from the Indian lines were falling from time to time on the Fort and a testy Manningham, anxious to waste no time, was incensed when Anna reached the ghat and saw her brother John with the soldiers. He stepped forward to embrace her, and in the haste and confusion neither probably had time to reflect that they might not set eyes on each other again. The children were lifted aboard, the small boat pushed off towards the *Dodaldy*, and soon those on the east curtain could see it no more.

Then Mary Carey, shepherding the second party down to the gate, came face to face with Manningham, who had planted himself by the river for the express purpose of making certain that no coloured women went aboard his vessel.

Mary had eleven whimpering, frightened children clutching at her skirts in the dark, and the need for haste was imperative. They had passed through the colonnade, and now they could see the budgerow held by two of Lushington's soldiers with the sailors ready to row them out into the river. The steps were slimy and treacherous. The mud oozed round them. The only light came from one lantern. And there, at the foot of the steps stood an implacable Manningham, who took one look at Mary Carey and flatly refused to allow her to take the children aboard.

Mary appears to have been more astonished than distressed. Every instinct prevented her arguing with a white man but she did apparently stammer out that she thought the chaplain had arranged something on her behalf. Manningham shouted almost hysterically, and in the midst of this angry scene, Lushington slipped away unnoticed to tell Lady Russell in the nursery, who appeared clutching her skirts as she ran down the colonnade to the water's edge to see what was amiss.

Lady Russell was afraid of nobody. Manningham, however, remained obdurate, and as the children were beginning to fret, Lady Russell announced that she would take this load to the *Dodaldy* but would return and take up the matter with the Governor. Mary meanwhile was sent back to look after the children who still remained in the nursery.

When one considers the near-chaos, the urgency, the desperate plight of the Fort, and the fact that Mary was British by marriage, it seems hardly credible that Manningham could be so inhuman, stubborn and obtuse; even for those days it seems unbelievably cruel. Yet Mary Carey was never to get on board, even though, after another angry scene, Lady Russell refused to leave the Fort unless she went. So bitter was the argument on Lady Russell's return that Mrs Dumbleton had to be sent for, and it was she who escorted the last group of children.

Hardly was the party aboard and the last boat about to cast off than one more person clambered aboard. It was Manningham, claiming that since thirty soldiers promised by Drake as a bodyguard had never arrived, the women were in urgent need of somebody in authority on the *Dodaldy* to make sure they came to no harm.

While the children were being evacuated at one gate, the women were assembling round the flagpole on the other side of Writers' Row. In order to avoid tearful and protracted farewells, no husbands were allowed through the passage other than Gervas Bellamy and Thomas, his eldest son, who was apparently causing the old man some anxiety. Sullen and morose, he was acting more strangely each day.

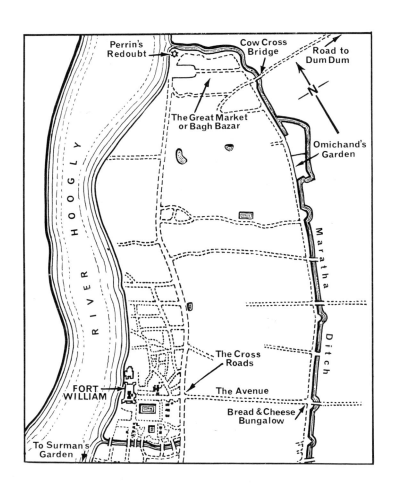

Perrin's Redoubt

Cow Cross Bridge

Road to Dum Dum

N

The Great Market or Bagh Bazar

Omichand's Garden

RIVER HOOGLY

Maratha Ditch

The Cross Roads

FORT WILLIAM

The Avenue

Bread & Cheese Bungalow

To Surman's Garden

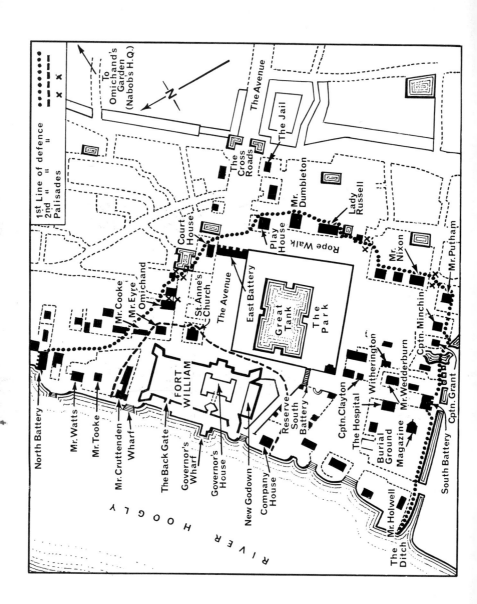

RIVER HOOGLY

North Battery
Mr. Watts
Mr. Tooke
Mr. Cruttenden
Wharf
The Back Gate
Governor's Wharf
Governor's House
New Godown
Company House

FORT WILLIAM

Reserve
South Battery

Cptn. Clayton
The Hospital
Witherington
Mr. Wedderburn
Cptn. Minchin
Cptn. Grant
South Battery

Burial Ground
Magazine
Mr. Holwell
The Ditch

Mr. Cooke
Mr. Eyre
Omichand
St. Anne's Church
Court House
The Avenue
East Battery

Great Tank
The Park

Play House
Rope Walk
Mr. Dumbleton
Lady Russell
Mr. Nixon
Mr. Putham

The Cross Roads
The Jail
The Avenue

To Omichand's Garden (Nabob's H.Q.)

N

1st Line of defence
2nd " "
Palisades

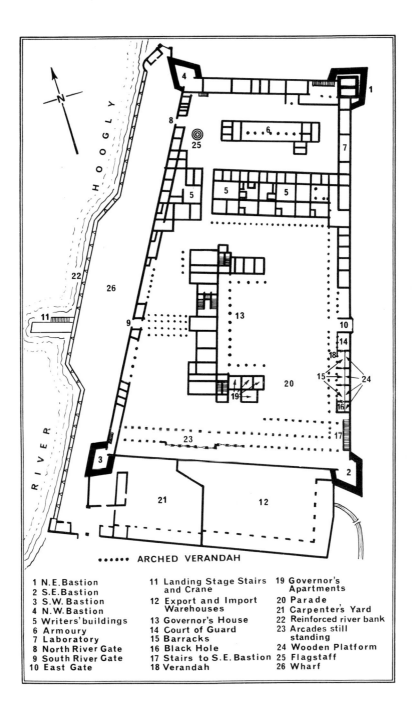

ARCHED VERANDAH

1 N.E. Bastion	11 Landing Stage Stairs and Crane	19 Governor's Apartments
2 S.E. Bastion	12 Export and Import Warehouses	20 Parade
3 S.W. Bastion		21 Carpenter's Yard
4 N.W. Bastion	13 Governor's House	22 Reinforced river bank
5 Writers' buildings	14 Court of Guard	23 Arcades still standing
6 Armoury	15 Barracks	
7 Laboratory	16 Black Hole	24 Wooden Platform
8 North River Gate	17 Stairs to S.E. Bastion	25 Flagstaff
9 South River Gate	18 Verandah	26 Wharf
10 East Gate		

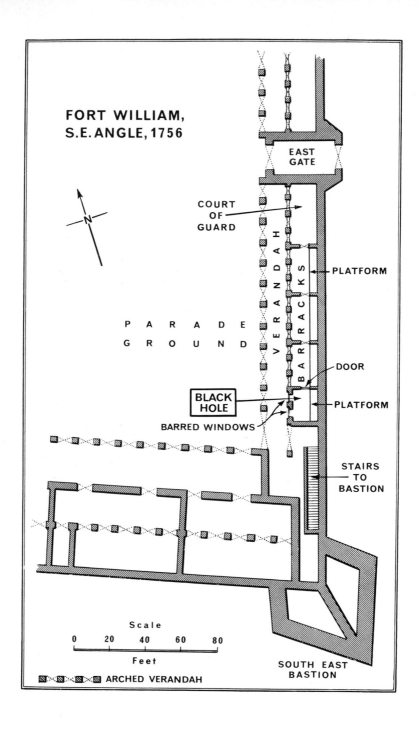

FORT WILLIAM,
S.E. ANGLE, 1756

N

EAST
GATE

COURT
OF
GUARD

V E R A N D A H

B A R R A C K S

PLATFORM

P A R A D E
G R O U N D

DOOR

BLACK
HOLE

PLATFORM

BARRED WINDOWS

STAIRS
TO
BASTION

Scale

0   20   40   60   80

Feet

ARCHED VERANDAH

SOUTH EAST
BASTION

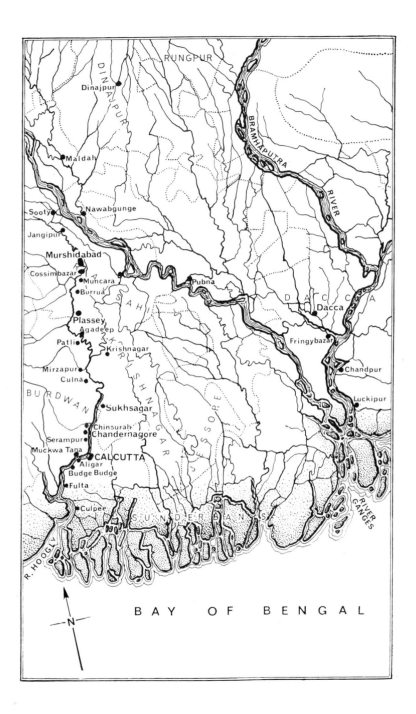

ABOVE
Panoramic view of Calcutta
LEFT
Siraj-Uddaula, Nabob of Bengal
RIGHT
John Zephaniah Holwell
Chief Magistrate of Calcutta

A contemporary view of Fort William, with the Governor's residence in the centre

The Black Hole (behind the barred window) with part of the barrack as seen from inside the verandah

FROM 'ECHOS FROM OLD CALCUTTA' BY H E BUSTEED

We have virtually no details of this evacuation, except one incident which occurred after Gervas had conducted a brief service at the flagpole, offering prayers for the safety of husbands and sons. The first boatload had already left for the *Dodaldy*, and Gervas and Thomas both assumed that every woman had left her cubicle; it was dark, the need for silence was imperative, and there must have been great disorder. The second budgerow was about to depart when Thomas heard someone moaning. The sound seemed to come from the end of the passage, and he pushed his way into room after room until at last he opened a door and saw a woman lying on her bed. It was Anne Mackett.

Thomas ran for his father, who stumbled back with a lantern. Mrs Mackett was lying naked on the bare straw. The old chaplain took one horrified look at the blood which covered both the bed and the unfortunate woman's inert body. Anne Mackett, the woman who never complained, had been left alone and had had a miscarriage. She must have been there for hours, the dead baby beside her, and had Thomas not found her she would certainly have bled to death. She was still alive, however, and Thomas shouted to two of the wives for help. They wrapped Mrs Mackett up in an old blanket and the men carried her to the gate and laid her in the last budgerow to leave, with the fourth and final party.

After Manningham's cowardly behaviour earlier that evening, it is hardly surprising to learn that Frankland had found it necessary to assert his authority by scrambling aboard this last boat.

Gervas and his son returned to the council chamber, where the situation was now swiftly deteriorating into chaos. Nobody—least of all Drake and Minchin—had any real idea of what was happening. We can gain some impression of what it was now like in the Fort from the account of William Lindsay, a twenty-one-year-old apprentice who had the honorary title of 'Assistant to the President'. Lindsay played no active part in the siege; he had lost a leg in some accident, and performed duties similar to those of an ambassador's social secretary. 'It is almost impossible', he wrote later, 'to conceive the confusion there was in the Fort, there being at least two thousand [native] women and children, nor was there any method to prevent them coming in as the military and militia declared they would not fight unless their families were admitted . . . The enemy began now to fire very warmly upon the Fort from all quarters. Our garrison began to murmur for want of provisions, having not a single cook in the Fort, notwithstanding there had been several lodged there on purpose to dress their provisions. The whole garrison was quite fatigued, having been under arms a great part of the preceding night. Many of the military and militia having got at liquor began to be very mutinous and under no command, having drawn bayonets on several of their officers.'

A large quantity of this liquor had been stocked in Writers' Row and the adjacent dining-hall, and almost before the evacuation was completed, the rumour spread that these quarters were now deserted. Scores of men who had not eaten for twenty-four hours were soon ransacking the rooms, smashing open cupboards, drinking anything they could find. It was the Dutch who proved the worst offenders, and two were shot when they attacked officers trying to stop the looting. Hedleburgh was arrested again, but was immediately freed when the other Dutch half-castes refused to fight until their sergeant was set at liberty.

As the drunkenness increased, the Dutch mercenaries started hunting for women among the refugees and there are many lurid (but obviously unsubstantiated) stories of young Indian girls being forcibly abducted from the parade-ground and taken to Writers' Row. Nevertheless, one is left in no doubt that this sort of thing certainly did happen on that fatal night.

For men like Holwell or even young officers like Blagg, used to instinctive discipline, order and obedience, the task of coping with troops on the verge of mutiny while the enemy was on the point of attacking the Fort again must have taxed their determination to the limit. The whole situation must have struck the few able and trustworthy officers left in the Fort as having developed into a prolonged and infinitely horrible nightmare. Nobody could be trusted—nobody from the Governor downwards. Drake was a broken, defeated man. Manningham and Frankland had disappeared; no one (at that time) knew where. In the outposts half the men were without food or water. On the parade-ground fighting spread rapidly among the refugees, who in themselves posed a fantastic problem at this crucial time. It is difficult to realize from this distance that, though the majority were poor, several rich Hindu merchants had forced their way into the Fort, not in rags and tatters but bringing with them their harems, children, stocks of food, and in some cases their slaves, who now guarded them zealously as the poorer, hungrier Hindus began to endeavour to snatch the food that was being eaten before their starving, envious eyes.

Apart from Holwell and Leach the carpenter, not a soul who toured the ramparts seems to have made any attempt to restore the morale of the troops or the civilians by at least announcing some plans for eventual evacuation. Any declaration, one feels, any resounding promise (even had it not been possible to keep it) might have stilled the ferment. Yet not a word ever came from the one man they might have looked to—the Governor, invisible, locked away in interminable and fruitless discussions in the Council, which broke up about ten o'clock that night without any decisions being made.

Even so, the Council had been shocked that evening when Drake irritably asked a messenger to fetch Colonel Manningham, who quite naturally was not to be found. Frankland's presence was then requested, but he could not be found either. One man then diffidently said that he had seen Manningham go aboard with the last party of children. Another interrupted to say that Frankland had gone aboard with the women.

Drake was stupefied. It was as though his best friend had betrayed him. Angrily he ordered an officer to take a boat to the *Dodaldy* and request them both to come to the council chamber immediately. The officer returned as quickly as possible and announced that Manningham and Frankland presented their compliments to the Governor, but felt that they owed it to the ladies to remain and guard them until the promised thirty soldiers arrived. Even worse, reports began to reach the Council that several members of the militia, including the Reverend Mapletoft, had somehow reached the *Dodaldy*. Each had refused to return. Their excuse was that Colonel Manningham, who was in charge, had ordered them to remain on board.

The effect of this news can be imagined. Drake became white with rage and walked across the council chamber to the window overlooking the Hoogly. Leaning out, he shook his fist at the shadows in the river, and as he did so someone cried that the lantern on the *Dodaldy* was moving.

It was indeed. Without any orders from the Fort, Manningham had decided to move the *Dodaldy* a little down-river, a short distance away from the other shipping. His excuse later was that he was afraid of the

Dodaldy being hit by fire-arrows, but since no other vessel was hit during the night, they must surely have been comfortably out of range of these primitive weapons. What Manningham obviously planned was to ensure that the *Dodaldy* was unencumbered by other shipping when the right moment arrived to make his escape.

The fury in the Fort when it became known that the *Dodaldy* had moved down-river exploded into a series of riots. Mutinous soldiers roamed the Fort, and several more officers were attacked. The *Dodaldy*, it is true, was still within range of the Fort and could easily be reached by budgerow. But once the news had spread that Manningham and Frankland were aboard, the sight of their ship moving away from the Fort aroused the worst kind of fears. For a tired, dispirited garrison, the sight could mean anything, and 'anything' aroused a natural fear and creeping suspicion that they were about to be abandoned.

There can be no doubt at all, as Holwell later pointed out in one of his long reports to the East India Company, 'that Messrs Manningham's and Frankland's falling down from the Fort with the *Dodaldy*, and refusing to return to it and join our councils the night of the 18th, though more than once summoned to it by your President, were the primary causes of all the confusion that ensued . . . The departure of the *Dodaldy* (of which these gentlemen were the part owners) and their refusal to return were the cause of jealousies and fears, which otherwise would never have existed.' It was a fact, said Holwell, that everything was 'sacrificed and abandoned to the consideration of these gentlemen's own safety. Had we remained united in our forces, and proper spirit shewn and examples made, what could have been apprehended from a few drunken Dutch soldiers or a few seditious among the rabble of the militia? [We] were surely more than equal to quell any tumult that could have been raised.'

And now just at a moment when the garrison's spirit was at its lowest, the Indians abandoned their normal tactics of not fighting after sunset and launched a series of sustained attacks on the Company House, just south of the Fort—the most vital of all the outposts since it prevented the enemy reaching the river and thus cutting off the garrison's escape route. Apparently the Nabob, incensed at the heavy losses, ordered his soldiers to fight in four-hour shifts, at the end of which time they were replaced by fresh troops.

Lieutenant Blagg was in command at the Company House, and about ten o'clock he sent a message that he could hold out no longer and requested permission to withdraw. Blagg must have been utterly exhausted, and for once Drake listened to Holwell, who urged an immediate retreat to the Fort before Blagg and his men were massacred. It was surely better, said Holwell, to save their lives for further fighting after they had rested.

It was a wise decision. Blagg succeeded in retreating to the Fort, but about midnight 'news was brought to us', said Lindsay, 'that the enemy was going to storm the Fort, there being ladders preparing close under the range of godowns [warehouses] to the southward; immediately every person repaired to the curtain where we absolutely heard them at work. Orders were now given to beat to arms but none of the Armenians or Portuguese appeared, having hid themselves in different parts of the Fort.' Grant said later that 'continual duty and want of refreshment so harassed both military and militia that . . . not a man could be brought on the ramparts, till dragged from the different corners of the Fort where they had retired to rest.'

The attack when it came cannot have been very heavy, however, for the European officers and the few men still available apparently managed to disperse the Moors by throwing hand-grenades from the southern curtain, 'which soon dislodged them'. And—quite unaccountably —the Moors made no attempt to occupy the Company House during the night.

Four of Blagg's men had been badly wounded in the fighting at the Company House, and, safely back in the Fort, had been carried to the ballroom, now transformed from a nursery into a makeshift hospital under the charge of Lady Russell and Mary. (Surgeon Gray seems to have been cut off at the hospital.) No bandages were available, but Lady Russell, without apparently asking the Governor, ransacked Mrs Drake's private apartments and took away all sheets, petticoats and other materials which could be torn up into strips.

It proved a disturbed night. Despite the temporary repulse, not a single practical plan seems to have emerged, although about two a.m., after the attacks on the southern warehouse had been beaten off, Drake called yet another war council at which non-Council members were present and 'everyone . . . was at liberty to give his opinion'.

Witherington was summoned, and Drake asked him bluntly how much powder was left. According to Drake, Witherington was 'first called upon to know the state of our ammunition, who reported that . . . there was no more left than sufficient for two days' firing, and that the greatest part thereof was damp and not fit for use until dried'.

This news—half expected by the more experienced, but apparently shattering information to Drake—exerted a profound effect on the council. For a moment the bald announcement stunned the meeting into silence; then everybody clamoured and cried, some in anger, others in disbelief; Drake banged on the table for quiet, but it was some time before the rage and fear subsided and the members re-seated themselves, mopping their brows against the heat of the night, and waiting dejected and crestfallen for the next item of bad news.

The news must have been horrifying, but at least it had one effect. At long last, after all the abortive wrangling, the frittering away of invaluable time, the almost total absence of a constructive attempt at planning, it brought every man in the council chamber face to face with one inescapable fact: without powder Fort William could not be held. The only alternative was a retreat to the boats.

But when? And how? Some wanted an immediate evacuation; others argued that were this plan to be allowed, the men in the outposts would have to be abandoned (which was probably right). And then there was the Company's treasure. Should it not take priority and be evacuated first of all? (Manningham and Frank-land, who were the treasurers and had the keys, were needless to say not available.) But thoughts of the treasure were set aside when it was pointed out that the tide was in flood and the high water would make it easier for the enemy to pick off men burdened by heavy boxes before they reached the ships. So the argument raged. Some were for evacuating the wounded immediately, others suggested waiting until the following day. Another group insisted that all refugees must be cleared out of the Fort, since otherwise the panic-stricken mob would make any attempt at an orderly withdrawal impossible.

Finally it was agreed that retreat to the ships should be postponed until the following night. There was still sufficient powder to enable the garrison to hold out throughout the coming day, and during that time the wounded could be evacuated so that the unencumbered garrison would be able to make a regular, orderly retreat after nightfall. Lindsay was rowed over to the *Dodaldy* to acquaint Manningham with this latest plan; he carried a personal message from the Governor insisting that no ships should be moved. Because of his lameness, he was told that he did not need to return to the Fort.

After Lindsay had left, Drake, apparently on a sudden impulse, asked Holwell to try and persuade Omichand to write to the Nabob. Holwell went to the Black Hole where Omichand was imprisoned with Kissendass, but, enraged at the treatment he had received, or else perfectly certain the Nabob was implacable, Omichand refused to co-operate, and remained in the comparative safety of the prison, nursing his wrath and biding his time.

Holwell had hardly returned with this information for Drake when an enemy cannon-ball scored a direct hit on the council chamber, crashing right through the room but causing no casualties. Its arrival, however, generated sufficient impetus for the Council to decide to wind up the meeting—which ended, according to Tooke, 'with the utmost clamour, confusion, tumult and perplexity, according to custom, without coming to any determination or resolution, but good-naturedly leaving every member to imagine his proposals would be followed and put into execution.'

By now, it was nearly dawn. The involved arguments had lasted for hours, and each survivor recounts the story of that dreadful night in different fashion, according to his temperament and indeed his memory, which varied greatly. All, however, are agreed on two points, whose significance is sometimes not fully realized.

First, it emerges that Drake was repeatedly urged to make some sort of announcement to the troops, in order to set aside their suspicions they might be abandoned and encourage them to fight on until the following dusk, so that the whole garrison might be safely evacuated. This he never did.

Second, it must never be forgotten that it was Drake himself who proposed that the garrison should fight on for one more day; it was Drake who promised to every man present that, given resolution and courage (and good leadership, he said), the Fort could be held until the following evening.

This being so, two things automatically happened when Drake later deserted. Because no announcement had been made, the bulk of the garrison was unaware of any plans for a general evacuation, and naturally imagined that the flight of the Governor marked the signal for a retreat to the ships. Those who *did* know the plans—those who had been at the meeting—now had first-hand evidence that Drake was not only a coward but a liar, a realization which no doubt inspired many to give up the struggle as hopeless and attempt to follow him.

The scene on the *Dodaldy* was one of complete confusion. Built to carry about fifty passengers, she was now crammed with nearly a hundred tearful women and whimpering children. Below decks the space was so crowded that Anna Bellamy and her mother could hardly turn around in the cramped cabin, twelve feet square, which nine women had to share.

They had nothing except the clothes they wore. Normally passengers embarking on an Indiaman brought all their own furnishings—a cot bedstead, mattress, pillows, blankets and bed linen, even a chest of drawers, washstand and footbath, as well as lamps or candles. None of these was available on the *Dodaldy* and in the turmoil of evacuation the women had brought nothing.

Most of them, after one look at their unsavoury surroundings below deck, preferred the fresh, if hot, air; but the decks too were crowded, partly with an assortment of animal life—ducks, turkeys, fowls, sheep, pigs, a cow and her calf—carried to provide fresh food until the time came when passengers would have to eat the pickled meat in barrels. The animals cluttered the decks; and since the *Dodaldy* was pierced for twenty-eight ninepounders, canisters of powder, ramrods, water buckets, cannon-balls and grape made movement on deck even more difficult.

The round-house on the upper stern deck had been partitioned by the ship's carpenter into cabins, including the captain's day cabin on the port side and his bed place to starboard. One cabin on the round-house was prepared for Anne Mackett to share with Sarah Mapletoft and her baby daughter; but the other women had to fend for themselves.

The master of the *Dodaldy* was Captain Andrew Young, a hard, ruthless Scot whose ship was his life. Like most captains of his day, he was permitted to carry considerable private cargo on each voyage and earned at least £5,000 a year. His authority was such that he could not be dismissed and could, when he wished to retire, sell his captaincy to any properly qualified master. He appears to have been a grim, forbidding man, tall, with thick iron-grey hair, enormous hands and a barrel chest. He never spoke, he roared his orders and insisted on rigorous discipline.

However laudable his concern for his vessel, Captain Young's feelings about the trapped garrison were soon to become brutally and inhumanly apparent. But then, he was not a man to waste time on sympathy, though, since Manningham and Frankland were part-owners of the *Dodaldy*, he had been unable to refuse to take the evacuees on board, however distasteful he found this flurry of petticoats.

It was just before dawn that Young became involved in the first of several unfortunate incidents, though it is difficult to piece together just what happened.

Peter Carey was serving on the *Dodaldy*, though he had been released, of course, to fight in the militia. Some time after midnight Peter boarded the *Dodaldy*, presumably to say farewell to Mary, for he knew nothing of what had happened. Mary, however, was nowhere to be found, and while searching for her he stumbled into Anna, who could not sleep.

Anna was as puzzled as Peter, for neither Mary nor Lady Russell had arrived; Mrs Dumbleton had told her there had been trouble with Manningham at the Governor's gate so Anna suggested to Carey that as Manningham was in the round-house he might discover from him what had occurred.

One can imagine the fearful scene which must have taken place in the round-house as Young's fury erupted when one of his own sailors burst in demanding that his coloured wife be brought aboard. In a few minutes Captain Young appeared at the top of the companionway gripping a struggling Carey. Anna saw Manningham behind him, holding a bottle, then Carey broke free and almost fell down on to the deck as Captain Young pulled his pistol out of his sash.

Carey picked himself up, darted past two sailors who tried to stop him, and before anybody realized what was happening, jumped on the gunwale. Anna had no time to stop him from diving into the river, and he started swimming for the bank. Captain Young fired twice into the darkness; then, without uttering a word, replaced his pistol in his sash and returned to the round-house.

In the darkness Carey swam back to the river bank,

and Blagg from his post in the Fort saw a shadowy figure stumble out of the water and shake itself like a dripping dog. He ran down to the water's edge, realized it was Peter Carey, and helped him back to the Fort, taking him straight to the hospital where Mary was sleeping.

It was just dawn on Saturday, June 19.

CHAPTER SEVEN

The Deserters

Saturday, June 19

The mist rose early after dawn on Saturday, and by the time the Fort was astir, the heat of the day was already pressing down. Almost immediately the guns of the enemy opened up from the east battery. All accounts agree that the fighting now reached its peak.

'By daybreak', says Tooke, 'the enemy began playing upon the church and Factory from two eighteen-pounders . . . and as all our endeavours to dispossess them of the houses proved ineffectual, and appearing in prodigious swarms all round the factory, struck a panic in many, expecting every moment the place would be stormed.'

'Things were found in a dreadful situation,' wrote Drake. 'At sunrise we perceived that a numerous body of the enemy was advancing on us from the eastward. They had in the night taken shelter from the battery quitted by Captain Clayton and had mounted cannon thereby.'

In the face of these ominous signs of mounting attack, Drake's subsequent behaviour seems almost incredible. Without telling anyone, he appears to have made his way to one of the passages under the parade-ground, where he promptly fell asleep. Nobody realized what had happened, nor could anybody find him. Consequently, he missed the bitter fighting which ensued and which now led to a momentous climax.

Shortly after dawn, Holwell had discovered that the enemy had not bothered to occupy the Company House from which Blagg had been forced to retreat during the night. It was astonishing that the Moors should have neglected such a tactically important point only forty yards south of the Fort, and Ensign Piccard immediately re-occupied it with twenty-five men.

Elsewhere, despite the fact that half of White Town was burning and 'at the same time the enemy's shot began to fly about the Fort', the outposts, though taking terrible punishment, were grimly holding on. Clayton's position in the church was being mercilessly battered by cannon from the east battery, while the small garrison in Eyre's house on the other side of The Avenue was also under constant fire. These two outposts, however, did not have the same tactical significance as Cruttenden's mansion and the Company House. Even if they fell, the enemy would still be faced with the task of either bombarding the Fort to ruins or scaling the walls, whereas Cruttenden's and the Company House commanded the river bastions and the stoutly built fences running from these bastions to the river bank—vital defence links if the garrison wished to keep the strip of land between the Fort and the river secure for their retreat after dark.

Unfortunately the enemy was well aware of the fact, and the Company House was the first to succumb under constant attack. Piccard fought against sustained assaults for two hours, but around nine-thirty the Nabob's troops launched an all-out attack in which four Britons were killed and Piccard, who had probably seen more fighting than anyone else, was badly wounded.

There was nothing for it but to retreat from the Company House once again. It was well-managed, covered by supporting fire from both southern bastions, though three more men were killed before the rest of the garrison gained the Fort. Piccard, however, was not with them. Badly wounded, he had sent his men out and remained alone. By all accounts he was a remarkably brave man. He had apparently been gashed in a shoulder and one leg, but now he managed to crawl across the compound and slither down the slimy steps of the wharf to the river bank. There his strength gave out and he was left for dead by the Indians—and by the British too, until Carey on the south-west bastion saw him make a slight movement, whereupon he rushed over to Lushington and requested permission to rescue Piccard.

Running down the steps to the Governor's gate, Carey waded into the Hoogly and started swimming down-river. The distance was not too far and he was a powerful swimmer. He came under heavy musket-fire, however, as soon as the enemy spotted him; nevertheless, he managed to reach Piccard, drag him into the water and start to swim back, supporting him. He had covered half the distance when he too was hit. Though the shoulder wound was superficial, it was enough to make him lose his grip on the wounded Ensign.

Lushington and two soldiers had by now run down to the Governor's gate. As soon as they saw the two men separate in the water, they leapt into a budgerow and by frantic rowing arrived just in time. Somehow they hauled the two wounded men aboard and the little party managed to reach the Fort safely, where Carey's wound was quickly dressed and Piccard was carried to Lady Russell's makeshift hospital in the Governor's ball-room.

The conditions in the hospital were by now appalling—the stench of the dead mingled with the retching and dysentery of the sick. There were no pots, pans or bowls, and men lay in their vomit or excrement. As more and more wounded were brought in, the room became so crowded that Mary Carey had to walk over the men lying on straw or the bare hard floor. On this day the surgeon, with few aids to assist him in saving lives, spent all morning amputating limbs, but almost every man died later. The dead were moved as quickly as possible but inevitably there were delays. The plight of the living must have been pitiful, for though they could and did moan with pain, none dared to speak except through scarcely opened lips because of the flies which settled everywhere, so that those who managed to eat a little rice prepared by Mrs Carey were too weary to brush them away and swallowed them in their food.

The loss of the Company House not only caused panic among the refugees and the coloured mercenaries in the garrison, but spurred the enemy on to greater effort. Within a short time the plight of the British became desperate. The Fort was under constant attack; fire-arrows were falling in ever-increasing numbers. The eighteen-pounders which Clayton had abandoned in the east battery had been turned round and were now employed in pounding the Fort and church with devastating effect.

The Moors grew bolder. One party managed to haul a field-piece across the churchyard and right up to the walls of the church, where they pushed the muzzle of the cannon through a window, opened fire at point-blank range and killed several men.

The effect was disastrous. Once again Clayton panicked; once again he retreated, abandoning his guns. At about the same time that he was falling back from the church, Lieutenant Blagg, who had held Cruttenden's house through the night, was attacked so heavily and continuously that by ten o'clock another five of his men had been killed. Unable to hold out any longer, he set fire to the house before retiring to the Fort.

Throughout this critical time, Drake was still sleeping and nowhere to be seen. In his absence, Minchin took it upon himself to issue orders. As soon as Cruttenden's fell, he made an important decision. Since three of the four outposts had now been abandoned, there was no point in holding out in Eyre's house; he ordered it to be evacuated too.

Yet though the enemy was now at times right beneath the walls as the fighting flared up, the position—if desperate—was by no means hopeless, for the evacuation of the wounded (including Lieutenant Lebeaume and Ensign Carstairs) was proceeding smoothly, and providing the Fort could resist for just one more day, there seemed no reason why the orderly withdrawal of the garrison could not take place as planned after nightfall. The evacuation of the outposts had in fact increased the fighting strength of the Fort. It was now simply a question of holding on.

The Moors had suffered such heavy losses that most of the garrison were determined to fight to the end, and though many of the half-caste troops were drunk there were still enough to resist all attempts to storm the Fort —especially with the knowledge that before another day had passed they would be safely aboard the ships.

The enemy had indeed suffered grievous losses, and though the estimates of casualties vary considerably, it does appear that over seven thousand were killed during the siege, and there is no doubt that Roy Doolub did not relish the prospect of making a direct frontal assault on the Fort.

As for the garrison, their only immediate danger lay in the chance that the enemy might attack the fences leading from the bastions to the river. Were these to be forced, all hope of retreat would be cut off. But two skilled ships' master-gunners had been placed in charge of the river bastions and those men who could be spared hastened to fill more sacks and bales of cotton-waste to close up as much as possible the dangerously wide embrasures.

The fighting must have been intense for the enemy 'galled the garrison in a terrible manner and killed and wounded a prodigious number', said John Cooke, Secretary to the Council, when giving evidence on the fall of Calcutta. Cooke (who survived the Black Hole) added, 'In order to prevent this havoc as much as possible, we got up a quantity of broadcloth in bales with which we made traverses along the curtains and bastions; likewise we fixed up some bales of cotton against the parapets to resist the cannon-balls and did everything in our power to baffle their attempt and hold out, if possible.'

The men laughed and sang as they undertook this unaccustomed work, and there was no reason to doubt their optimism; for Holwell was shortly to prove that the Fort could be held for twenty-four hours, even after scores of men had deserted.

But the day was hot. It seemed to drag on into infinity, and one vital force was still urgently needed to sustain courage and resolution during the hours that lay ahead—the inspiration of leadership. This was completely lacking.

During the evacuation of the outposts, Drake had slept. The more charitable say he had fallen asleep after inspecting the maze of damp passages linking the rooms and warehouses beneath the parade-ground; that on his way back, he had seated himself on a wooden chest by the stairway leading up to his residence and remembered nothing until he was suddenly brusquely awakened. It was here that Lieutenant Witherington, in charge of the powder-train, found him. He had first gone to Drake's personal apartments and now, as he descended the stairs, caught sight of the Governor sitting awkwardly on a chest just as he had fallen asleep, with his head slumped forward. Near-by were several refugee women who had crept there for shelter.

This meeting between Drake and Witherington was to change the entire fortunes of the garrison. It was the most crucial single moment of the siege and it is not difficult to imagine the setting and the drama—the dank, rat-infested passageway, with Drake barely visible in the half-light; the chattering, frightened women, children at their breasts; the weak, indolent Witherington timidly approaching, yet hardly daring to wake the Governor who was still blissfully unaware that in a matter of seconds disaster awaited him. One can imagine Witherington touching the Governor on the shoulder, waking him with a start; and Drake perhaps rubbing his eyes and asking where he was, what was happening. It is believed Witherington whispered something in his ear, but Drake—still half asleep—cannot have understood and probably snapped at the terrified Witherington to speak more plainly. When Witherington repeated his information it was loud enough to be overheard.

And then one can imagine Drake's stupefaction, his gasp of horror as he realized the full import of what Witherington was babbling and stammering about. There had been a miscalculation . . . nobody was to blame . . . but the estimates were wrong . . . and—well (one can imagine Witherington's terror) the truth was . . . there was no more dry powder.

Before Drake could jump up or even cry out, one of the Hindu women screamed, and ran stumbling for the stairway of packed, smooth mud. Drake lunged forward to stop her—obviously she must know enough English to have understood what had been said—but he was not quick enough. As she darted off to spread the news around the parade-ground, Drake rounded on Witherington.

Witherington, however, was telling the truth. There *was* powder, but apart from the supplies already issued to the garrison, almost all of it was damp and useless.

Drake groped his way upstairs, the urgent need to avert a panic burning in his mind, but by the time he reached the council chamber, everybody on the parade-ground already seemed to know, and as he wrote later in his defence statement, 'now appeared the utmost horror amongst the women in the factory, running to and fro with their children, many suckling at the breast'. As the horrified watchers in the council chamber looked out helplessly, they saw hundreds of women rise spontaneously like a wave, and surge across the parade-ground, running, stumbling, fighting, kicking, shrieking, as they fought their way to Writers' Row and escape through the back gate. Nothing could stop the flood of women as they rushed into the bottleneck of the small alley. The two sentries at the small passage were trampled to death.

It is doubtful if Drake could have done anything to stem the panic, but he was never even to have the opportunity. For as he stood there, Grant dashed up shouting that the enemy from the Company House was trying to force the river fence under the south-west bastion. Every man rushed to the bastion, which was under heavy musket-fire from the superior height of the Company House. Drake asked almost hysterically for Captain Minchin, but Minchin was nowhere to be found.

It was a desperate situation. Scores of Indians were crowding against the gate in the vital fence. Yet it was impossible for the garrison of the bastion to fire down on them, for the second a man stood up, he became exposed to heavy musket-fire from the Company House. The pandemonium and confusion must have been incredible, until one lucky cannon shot from the bastion started a fire in the Company House. Surprised and stunned, the enemy there ceased firing and immediately this happened, every man in the bastion stood up and fired down on the throng below. Before the Indians in the Company House could put out the fire and get to their muskets again, the attack had been beaten off, but in that short vicious struggle, the British lost nineteen men—eleven killed and eight wounded. Indian losses were put at over a hundred.

Now everything seemed to happen simultaneously. As the last of the Moors fled from the fence an officer in the bastion pointed up-river. Startled, smoke-grimed faces stared in the direction of his hand. It was an un-nerving sight. Scores of women were flooding out of the back gate towards an old passenger boat, one nor-mally used for ferrying.

Like a phalanx, the solid mass of women charged down the steps to the water. Some tried to steal the few small boats that still remained, but the majority, imagining that safety lay in size, made for the larger vessel. Holding their children above their heads, they struggled and waded waist-deep into the river to reach her. At least two hundred women and children managed to board the ship which had been built to take a maximum of fifty people, and when she started to drift slowly down-river, she left behind a piteous crowd of imploring women standing in the water.

The men in the Fort could see some of them begging for help as they stood in deep water trying to climb over the gunwales, only to be viciously attacked by those women already on board. Holwell and Gervas Bellamy, who had rushed to the west curtain, saw the ancient Indian vessel slowly glide away; then, just when it seemed that this one boatload at least would be saved, the Indians near Cruttenden's flaming house loosed off volley after volley of fire-arrows.

The first arrows fell short, hissing among the screaming women wading in the river, but soon new volleys were reaching their target and a spiral of smoke was seen rising from the deck. Without warning it burst into flames. Within seconds the frantic cargo of women and children became trapped in an inferno.

Almost everything that happened could be seen by those on the west curtain of the Fort. As the vessel drifted past, women with their children, their garments on fire, leapt into water too deep for them to hope to survive, presumably choosing in their last moments a death by drowning rather than by fire.

Suddenly the blazing ship lurched; she seemed to quiver and shake, and then heeled over so that the women clinging to the sloping burning deck fell off as the vessel began to slither under the water. An extract from a letter written from Chandernagore said that 'those who were eye-witnesses of this confusion counted the number they saw drowned at more than two hundred people.'

In 'this confusion' nobody had given a thought to Captain Minchin, but now it was suddenly discovered that not only the commander but several officers had vanished. Although the soldiers manning the walls stood firm, the chaos elsewhere in and around the Fort must have been such that at first nobody really appreciated what was happening. Drunken troops staggered across the parade-ground. One Portuguese drew a sword on John Bellamy when ordered to his post. The wailing refugees were streaming back into the Fort, clashing head-on with drunken troops trying to reach the river. Below the west wall of the Fort, the steps were crammed with troops trying to desert, and the river bank was choked with shouting, yelling men and women, all impelled by the urge to run away—anyhow, anywhere. One thought must have been in every man's brain: the powder had given out.

Holwell apparently bumped into Drake, who was still crying hysterically to nobody in particular for Minchin. The situation must have seemed hopeless. St Jacques's cannon were battering the Fort and a new and heavy fire was coming from the enemy guns installed in the Company House. Fire-arrows seemed to be falling everywhere; yet in the havoc nobody seemed to bother about the enemy fire; most people were too preoccupied with their own welfare.

As Drake and Holwell leaned over the parapet looking down on the river, they saw the Governor's private ghat crammed with Europeans, including several officers fighting to get into the few remaining budgerows. Half a dozen small boats lay stuck in the mud of the river bank, and as some of the shouting officers and men pushed off, Captain Grant dashed up and pointed to a boat some way beyond the steps. There—before their astonished eyes—was Captain Minchin clambering aboard a budgerow. While Drake and Holwell watched him helplessly, others, too, noticed what was happening and began shouting. O'Hara, the engineer, climbed in after Minchin and seized the oars. Why he deserted has never been explained. A cry of fury rose from the ramparts and for a full minute Drake stood there, unable to believe what he saw. Then he started to run to the Governor's gate. Grant followed him.

Gervas Bellamy was standing close to Holwell. Both

saw the Governor climb down the steps on to the river bank and force his way through the crowd. Every man on the ramparts watched to see if Drake would be in time to stop Minchin—it cannot have entered anybody's head that Drake was on the river bank for any other purpose.

O'Hara, pulling strongly, was rowing straight for the *Dodaldy* as Drake reached a point on the bank perhaps fifty yards north of the Governor's gate. Still the truth never occurred to the watchers on the ramparts, and even when their own eyes told them what was happening, it seemed impossible to believe. Alone on the mud-flats stood a budgerow guarded by an Indian with a drawn scimitar. A watching soldier suddenly realised that it was the Governor's own boat.

If they were going to catch Minchin, every second was precious. But Drake, with Grant hard at his heels, seemed to hesitate as he reached it, and soon every man on the ramparts could plainly see Grant gesticulating and arguing. It was obvious the two men were quarrelling. It must have been a considerable quarrel for they were still arguing there as Minchin's budgerow reached the *Dodaldy*. Both he and O'Hara could be seen, two small figures in the sunlight, being helped aboard.

Suddenly Drake appeared to threaten Grant and then the Indian with the scimitar jumped out of the budgerow, waded into shallow water, and pulled it off the mud. Now Drake splashed ankle-deep into the water as the Indian held the small boat steady. With some difficulty he clambered aboard. Grant hesitated—and then he too waded into the water and jumped into the boat. Before anybody had time to realize what was happening, before they had time to believe what they saw, Drake's servant was rowing straight for the *Dodaldy*. Drake never looked back.

After the first moment of stunned disbelief, the men on the ramparts shouted, shook their fists, and, as Tooke reported, 'upon the Governor's going off, several muskets were fired at him', adding with a rare flash of humour, 'but none were lucky enough to take place.'

But down on the river bank where considerable numbers of soldiers were milling around, the situation must have seemed less clear-cut. Not a man down there was aware that no order had been issued for a retreat. They had seen the Governor and the garrison commander making for the boats, and naturally assumed that because they were outside the Fort they had missed the order. There was an immediate stampede for the few remaining boats, and several men were killed in severe fighting between Europeans and refugees.

Before anybody else could reach the *Dodaldy*, however, the Governor had boarded her and almost immediately she started to move a little way down-river, and 'upon Mr Drake's ship getting under sail', wrote Tooke, 'every ship followed his example, and in less than an hour's time not a boat was to be seen near the factory, nor a vessel in condition to move'.

So on that hard, hot morning, shortly before noon, in one of the most inglorious episodes in the history of the East India Company, the leaders of a besieged garrison fighting against incredible odds brutally deserted them and deprived them of their only means of escape.

Out of the original garrison of five hundred and fifteen Europeans pitted against fifty thousand Indians, only a hundred and seventy now remained, and for them the siege was resolved into a starkly simple issue. It was no longer a test of strength against a despot wishing to curtail British rights; it was no longer a bitter personal quarrel between two men of petty minds; it had never been a war of passion against a foe they had hated.

Now it was a simple problem: a battle for survival.

One historical point must be made here. Altogether, over fifty Europeans deserted. Yet in justice it should be recorded that many of them did so unknowingly. Nothing can mitigate the conduct of Drake and Minchin, nor the even more evil and deliberate machinations of Frankland and Manningham. But there is no doubt that several Europeans must honestly have believed that they had missed the order to retreat. How else can one explain the behaviour of Grant, who had proved himself a fine fighting man and an excellent adjutant? Holwell himself spoke up in his defence when his actions were debated by the court of directors of the East India Company.

Grant himself described later how he had seen Drake standing by his private boat 'beckoning to his servant' and believed that he was instructing him to make sure the boat was securely tied up to prevent any natives stealing it. But suddenly, according to Grant, the Governor jumped aboard. Grant actually tried physically to stop Drake, but the Governor tore himself free, and 'I earnestly entreated he would first acquaint the garrison of his designs. He represented the impossibility of making a regular retreat.' Grant then seems to have come to the conclusion he could best serve the garrison by following the Governor in the hope of persuading him not to abandon the Fort. 'My station of adjutant-general', he argued, 'had fixed me to no particular post in the Fort, but more properly was to attend the Governor for his orders and act in a manner as his aide-de-camp.' If this excuse sounds a little hollow, there is no doubt that once on board the *Dodaldy*, Grant did try his utmost (though without any result) to persuade the Governor and Captain Young to move the ships up close to the Fort.

A very different case deserves special mention. William Mackett had been given permission to visit the *Dodaldy* on two occasions to see Anne, who was still desperately ill after her miscarriage. On the Friday he had gone to console her in the cabin she shared with Sarah Mapletoft and had refused Manningham's suggestion to remain on board. 'He left her dangerously ill about eleven and returned to the Fort,' wrote Holwell, 'though the strongest persuasions, I am informed, were used to detain him on board. But he returned to the duty his honour called him to with the consent and approbation of Mrs Mackett. Early on the morning of the 19th . . . Mr Mackett intimated to me the unhappy condition in which he left his lady, and expressed his desire to step on board for five minutes to see her. That this was [his] sole motive I am convinced of.'

When Drake came aboard and immediately ordered Captain Young to move down-river Mackett was trapped, but he later made the most strenuous efforts to return to shore, offering (in vain) a thousand rupees to anybody who would get him one of the ship's boats so that he could row himself back.

In Fort William, all the remaining Europeans now flocked to the council chamber. Now the peril was so acute and all hope seemed lost, they seemed to have come together by instinct, impelled by some deep-rooted longing for the one element they had always so far lacked —leadership. Never before had they been in such desperate need of a leader. They found one in Holwell.

The senior official in that meeting of lost souls was Paul Pearkes, the Company's chief accountant, but it appears that the assembled soldiers and militia forcibly demanded that Holwell be their leader and after some argument Pearkes agreed to step down, a minute being entered in the books to this effect. Drake and Minchin were formally suspended, and it is intriguing to reflect that, with all the fighting around them, there was still time and opportunity for a council meeting conducted on strictly formal lines, with the minutes kept in longhand. (Possibly it was nearing midday and the fighting had slackened, according to custom.)

After denouncing the action of the Governor and garrison commander, Holwell swore to fight to the end and immediately announced news that caused all in the council chamber to stand and cheer.

There was good reason—for despite their desperate situation there remained one lifeline which might lead to safety amid the despair engendered when all the vessels opposite the Fort had moved down-river. Everybody seemed to have forgotten that the *Prince George* was still anchored opposite Perrin's Redoubt, where her master, Captain Hague, had assisted Ensign Piccard so enthusiastically in the first battle of the siege.

Holwell now told them he would send a message to Captain Hague, requesting him to sail down-river to a point opposite the Fort. Once there, Hague was to remain out of range of fire-arrows until dusk. As soon as it grew dark he would sail close in towards Fort William and take off the garrison.

The tonic effect of this news must have been electric, and coupled with it was the new and heartening realization that at last here was a real leader—a man who told them the truth, issued clear orders instead of making vague promises, demanded sacrifices, but was prepared to die with them. Above all, here was a man who inspired hope, who was to produce one of those moments of history when men, impelled by some deep (and one is tempted to say mystical) emotion, suddenly behaved in a

manner entirely unexpected and fought with a bravery
the garrison as an entity had never previously displayed.

It is true they were fighting for their lives. It is also
true that the prospect of safety provided a magical spur.
But Holwell's influence on the garrison went deeper
than that and exerted a profound effect on men who a
few hours before (with an even greater prospect of safe
delivery) had sullenly refused to obey orders but now
were to fight like madmen.

There were doubtless other influences at work too—
fury at what had happened, at the manner in which they
had been deserted. The chain-reaction of a calamity can
produce strange consequences in the minds of ordinary
men, and though nobody can tell what they were thinking,
they were probably motivated by a desire for revenge
against those who had deserted them.

It was leadership combined with shame and revenge,
not fear, that drove them forward now. Until this morning all the qualities vital to stimulate flagging men had
been pitifully lacking. Now Holwell was in command.
He was no soldier, but it did not matter. He was not
particularly liked (he was too severe to encourage many
friendships), but that did not matter either. In the inde-
finable way that leaders throughout history have inspired
men to fight against insuperable odds, Holwell was able
to inspire the tiny, disorganized rabble that was his army
with his own faith, the token of inspiration—a sign, a
cause, a symbol, a flag—that will always compel men to
die willingly.

One wonders what Holwell's thoughts were at this
one great moment of his life when he surveyed the disorganized forces so unexpectedly under his command.
Holwell wrote a great deal after the siege, but though he
gave lucid reasons for the causes of defeat, he was
curiously reticent about his own thoughts. His early

training as a surgeon, followed by his career as a magistrate, may between them have inhibited him; when he
wrote about others he could be angry, reproachful or
laudatory; but (except in his narrative of the Black Hole)
his reports of the siege have the impersonal quality of a
barrister's brief, and his suggestions of what should have
been done are as dispassionate as a doctor's prescription.
Though he fought throughout the siege and lived
through the Black Hole, when he came to write about it,
it was as though he were an outsider looking in.

It must have been a strange moment when he was
elected, standing there, hand clenched on the butt of his
pistol, his hands torn and bleeding, his shirt filthy, in
the tattered clothes of a common soldier, commander of
a starving deserted army of men in rags, his audience
the half-naked Hindus, their wives and crying children;
yet none who saw him on that morning doubted that,
though destiny had placed him in a field of action of
which he knew nothing, his defiance and energy would
be an inspiration to them all.

Forming the officers and men into two groups, Holwell addressed them briefly. He told them the truth.
Mr Pearkes was to leave immediately with the message
for Captain Hague, but everything depended on their
ability to hold out till dusk. If the puny garrison could
fight for the rest of the day, there was no reason why
the whole garrison should not be safely evacuated on the
Prince George. As an added encouragement to the men,
he ordered three chests of treasure to be shared out. It
was the first time since the siege started that the men
had been assembled; the first time they had been given
real information by any responsible authority.

Holwell acted swiftly. Pearkes was sent off in a
budgerow which had been hidden under the Governor's
ghat. Two sailors rowed him briskly out of range of the

fire-arrows, and then began the long pull a mile and a
half up-river to the *Prince George*.

As though fortune were favouring his plans, the
Indians' fire now died down, and with the fighting
virtually at a standstill, Holwell was able to make a tour
of the entire Fort. He proved indefatigable. He did not
make extravagant promises to men who were almost
starving, but set about solving every vital physical
difficulty which Drake and Minchin had either ignored
or left to others.

The most urgent need was for food. For two days
nobody had eaten anything but hard biscuits—not because of shortage of food but for the incredible reason
that there were no pots or pans in which to cook the
rice and wheat. Holwell immediately commandeered a
supply from the richer refugees who (as already noted)
were in some cases surrounded on the parade-ground by
their harems and personal guards of slaves. The magistrate dealt ruthlessly with the slightest opposition. When
the guards of one protesting Armenian became aggressive, the Armenian was shot where he stood.

Old furniture from Writers' Row was soon being
broken up for fires which were lit near the armoury,
away from the refugees, and here Mary Carey, helped
by Lady Russell, started cooking large pans of rice and
making *chapattis*, or Indian bread, and tea. The troops
were fed in relays in orderly fashion in the adjacent
Company dining-hall. It was their first hot meal since
the start of the siege.

There was still a fair amount of drunkenness, but in
order to discourage men from searching for liquor (and
fighting for it, instead of fighting for the Fort), Holwell
issued dependable officers with liberal rations of arrack
to give the men tots from time to time.

Next he reorganized the powder supplies. As the

number of defenders had shrunk, there was now more powder for the remaining men, and Holwell reckoned that, husbanded carefully, there would be sufficient to hold out for the day. It was divided up, and a third was issued to responsible officers for the musketeers; the rest went to the four bastions.

Around three o'clock, the midday lull was broken as the Moors attacked again with renewed violence. For the first time they now made a serious attempt to scale the walls. Using bamboos placed against the east curtain, they started clambering up 'with an agility scarce to be believed' and men had to be rushed from all over the Fort to repel the attack.

At last the Indians fell back, having suffered appalling losses. But the garrison had not gone unscathed. In order to fire down from the parapets on the men swarming up the walls they had been exposed to enemy musket-fire from the church and Eyre's house. Five British defenders were killed and fourteen injured, of whom several died later.

But at least the garrison was fighting now with magnificent courage and optimism. This particular attack was beaten back without mercy, and the Indians were fleeing across The Park (with the British impatiently holding their fire) when three soldiers, yelling wildly, ran across the parade-ground. The *Prince George* had just come into view. She could be plainly seen from the riverside curtain sailing slowly and serenely in mid-river towards the Fort.

It is not difficult to picture the moment this news reached the Fort. Now that the Indians were in full retreat, half the garrison, it seems, raced across the parade-ground, all discipline forgotten in the sudden surge of excitement and hope. But it must have been a poignant moment too, for many hours of fighting still lay before them. Yet now the tired, unwashed men could actually see tiny figures moving on the decks of the *Prince George*—men who knew nothing of the conditions in which the garrison was fighting, but who lived in another world of good food, cleanliness and, above all, comparative safety.

The *Prince George* was still some way off and there was no time for long-drawn-out celebrations, for the Indians soon launched another heavy attack, supported by several newly-placed cannon. The enemy gunners were nothing if not enterprising and the eighteen-pounders which Clayton had abandoned had now been hauled forward from the east battery and were firing from positions on The Avenue. (These guns, in fact, did more damage to the Fort than any others.) Another battery had been placed at the south-west corner of The Park, from where the enemy maintained steady fire on the two southern bastions; three field-pieces had been dragged into the church after its evacuation, and this not only provided them with excellent cover, but the church was so well constructed that the British guns could not demolish it.

As always, however, the greatest danger came from the small-arms fire in the high buildings which the Moors were occupying close to the Fort. From these vantage points they were able to fire down continuously on the defenders, making it almost impossible for them to move along the walls. Despite this, the British several times throughout the afternoon managed to sally out and dislodge the enemy from Cruttenden's, Eyre's and the Company House. Each time, however, they were forced to fall back and the houses were soon re-occupied by fresh Indian troops.

As the fighting continued, one chance shot from the north-west bastion scored a direct hit on Cruttenden's house. It was a crucial moment. The grape fell into the midst of a mass of Indians. Alone, this might not have been remarkable, but almost simultaneously another cannon-ball from the north-east bastion hit the house. Already filled with dead and wounded, moaning men, Cruttenden's now caught fire, and—demoralized by two successive blows—the remaining Moors fled, abandoning their wounded. Before new forces could re-occupy the place, the old timbers and the roof, dry as tinder before the monsoon, had turned Cruttenden's into a furnace, roasting the wounded who could not escape.

This news soon flashed across the Fort and the gunners redoubled their cannonade on Eyre's and the Company House. Holwell seemed to be everywhere, spurring on the men. The Indian panic spread—just how, it is impossible to say—but suddenly it was as though the tide had turned and, despite the incredible disparity in numbers, the initiative actually passed for a short spell to the garrison. Had they not been under the strictest orders to conserve their powder, they could have done much more damage.

As it was, for a time confused groups of Indians could be seen running around aimlessly. Strangely enough, the enemy in Eyre's house seemed under the impression that their own troops had set fire to Cruttenden's house to prevent the British occupying it. Consequently they now abandoned Eyre's house. And then, suddenly, the Company House was emptied too. In a matter of minutes, the three houses that had, together with the church, caused the British such grievous trouble and loss of life were empty and burning, and three gushing, writhing plumes of smoke reassured the British that never again would a murderous small-arms fire pour down on them from houses whose roofs and windows overlooked the Fort walls.

The effect was immediate. Not only could the garrison now move freely about the Fort, but the danger of an attack on the two fences linking the eastern bastions with the river had suddenly receded. Now only the church, fifty yards away, commanded the Fort.

It was about this time—just when the surge of excitement was stirring the garrison to even greater efforts— that tragedy struck Gervas Bellamy. The old chaplain worked and fought magnificently. He was with Holwell and his officers now, discussing plans for the retreat, when an officer entered the room and whispered to the new commander. Those near him saw the dismay on the magistrate's face. Nerves were so edgy that there was an instant clamour for information. Holwell assured them there was no cause for worry. He turned to the chaplain and spoke quietly to him.

The message concerned Bellamy's elder son Thomas, and all we can be certain about is contained in the unfeeling official sentence: 'Thomas Bellamy shot himself on the walls.' We know from his father that he was a moody, introspective man. He does not appear to have been afraid. He had never contemplated desertion when the opportunity was there. At one moment he was apparently fighting on the east curtain; the next, he stood up—which in itself meant certain death—and before the enemy could fire, put his pistol to his head and pulled the trigger.

The story of the siege of Calcutta is one in which, even allowing for the blunders of its leaders, bad luck—sheer misfortune—seems to have dogged the defenders each time they appeared near to overcoming disaster. Now, about five o'clock, when everything seemed to be going so well, when hopes were higher than they had been since the morning, when enemy attacks had been beaten back, a new disaster—the one stroke of bad luck nobody ever envisaged—befell the Fort. The *Prince George*, upon which everything now depended, ran aground on a sandbank.

The news shattered the morale of the garrison. Here was an accident that must have made them wonder in their dismay if even the Lord had not abandoned them. And indeed, in the whole story of the siege, it is not the blunders and crass incompetence for which blame can be apportioned, but the almost uncanny succession of unaccountable misfortunes which makes it seem as though Fort William lay under some inexplicable and preordained curse. The run of ill-luck was so persistent that had it been incorporated in a work of fiction, the novelist would be criticized for clumsily contriving situations in order to heighten the drama. Yet all these events actually occurred in unrelenting sequence, with disastrous results which the unhappy garrison could hardly foresee even in their worst nightmares.

What had caused the latest catastrophe? Navigation on the Hoogly was so dangerous that pilots were always employed, and by another stroke of misfortune, the pilot who normally guided Captain Hague was ill and a Dutchman named Francis Morris had taken his place. And Morris, who enters the story for only a few critical minutes, panicked.

One moment the *Prince George* was sailing smoothly down-river to her rendezvous, a point in mid-river exactly opposite the Fort, when suddenly the wind freshened and before anybody—least of all Morris, who should have taken precautions against such an event— realized what had happened, the *Prince George* had slewed round and was making straight for the river bank.

Captain Hague yelled to the lascars to take in sail, but his crew, terrified of approaching the Fort and apparently believing the *Prince George* was now going alongside in daylight, panicked too. One can imagine their horror as the outline of the Fort loomed larger and they could see the raging fires that ringed it and hear the cannon of the Nabob whose very name inspired terror. Without warning, they began to jump overboard, preferring drowning to the tortures they were convinced the Nabob would inflict should they fall into his hands.

With his lascars gone it was impossible for Captain Hague to trim the sails. But the *Prince George* was still out of range of the fire-arrows—by far the biggest danger to shipping—and Captain Hague seized the wheel from Morris and partly succeeded in bringing her round. The Dutch pilot—the only man who knew the position of the sandbanks—lay cowering on the deck at a moment when his knowledge of the river was most urgently needed. Hague could not be expected to know the treacheries of the Hoogly, but when the British sailors climbed into the rigging and started to trim sail, he managed to bring the *Prince George* almost to a standstill. But not quite. Without warning, she lurched and shuddered; and as the vessel hit a sandbank the Captain was thrown across the deck, leaving the wheel spinning behind him. Three sailors in the rigging were tossed overboard and never seen again.

The *Prince George* was listing now but she was not holed. One hope remained. Picking himself up, Hague decided to use his anchor in an endeavour to refloat her. Every available man rushed to the windlass and the cable rattled down. Twice they almost pulled her off. Each time the *Prince George* shivered Hague hoped she would move, but the truth was that one anchor was not sufficient.

Still the gallant Captain Hague refused to give in. The *Prince George* carried only one anchor—and it was almost, but not quite strong enough to pull the vessel off the bank. A second anchor would unquestionably provide just the extra required impetus. And there was a second anchor available—on the *Dodaldy*, the only ship in the fleet that carried a spare anchor and cable.

Equipped with that vital anchor, it seems certain that the *Prince George* could have been refloated and that every man in the Fort could still have been evacuated. All that was necessary now was to borrow an anchor from the *Dodaldy*. A sailor was rowed over to her immediately. And there, incredibly, his request was met with a flat refusal from Captain Young. Even more disturbing was the fact that Drake refused to intercede, nor would Manningham and Frankland help in any way, even though (or possibly, because) they were part-owners of the vessel.

Captain Young's reasoning was simple: his charges were so important that he could not be responsible for the risk. Captain Grant tried to influence the Governor and Captain Young, but was told not to interfere.

One can imagine the scene on board when the women heard of Young's decision; the waiting women with their whimpering children, trapped on a vessel whose master would not even lend an anchor to save their men. It is hard to believe, for as Tooke wrote, their behaviour was 'something so scandalous and inhuman that it is a reflection upon the nation. When they were informed that the Company's ship [the *Prince George*] was run ashore, but might be got off with the assistance of an anchor and cable, and might also be the preservation of the lives of those who were left in the garrison, even that was refused being sent, though they had sufficient belonging to their ship to have done it and not distressed themselves in the least . . . was it not their duty to run some little risk for the preservation of so many lives; such an unprecedented affair surely is not to be paralleled amongst the greatest barbarians, much more among Christians.'

The refusal stands out as the most inhuman act recorded throughout the whole siege, for Captain Young would have taken virtually no risk in lending the anchor. Even worse is the fact he could undoubtedly have been persuaded to change his mind had the Governor thought fit to intercede. No wonder Tooke added that the deaths which followed could be laid to Drake and Manningham as plainly 'as if they had cut their throats; because they not only acted basely in quitting the garrison and carrying away the shipping, but actually had it in their power to have saved every man's life afterwards.'

So the last hope of saving the garrison now vanished, for every man there was able to see the final moments of the *Prince George* for himself. Within the hour, a small boat filled with Indians had plundered her. Soon they set her on fire so that she blazed for hours, far into the night.

Now only two alternatives were left—an honourable death or capitulation. The younger members of the garrison, it seems, remained undaunted and when one remembers that most of them were hardly more than boys—and fighting in a humid heat of around a hundred degrees—it is hard to imagine that any courage remained. But now that the last hope of retreat was cut off, the mood of the garrison for the most part understandably changed. The remarkable morale that had sustained them all day—based too firmly on the false hope of retreat—was inevitably doomed to disintegration. The cost in lives had been heavy; during the day nineteen men had been killed. The mood of the mercenaries—the

Portuguese, Armenians and particularly the Dutch half-castes—grew uglier with each passing hour, until by nightfall all the magnificent discipline which had distinguished and sustained them throughout the day was gone and drunken gangs were rampaging again. Holwell was confronted with a recurrence of the old problem. Man after man, desperate and exhausted, fell to looting the deserted officers' quarters for drink, or fighting with the refugees for women. They tore open lockers, smashed the necks of bottles of madeira, arrack, brandy, and with lips bloody from the jagged edges, gulped down a bottle at a time. Already exhausted, many were dead drunk within the hour. The younger officers—Blagg, Bellamy and others—found them everywhere; flat on their backs, snoring, vomiting, some giggling with tension, but the majority of them incapable. On the ramparts one laughing man, a bottle to his lips, threw himself over the parapet. Another shot a sentry at the river gate and, singing loudly, walked into the Hoogly up to his knees, toppled over, and was never seen again. Those who still retained some semblance of discipline seemed physically unable to obey orders. A soldier was seen trying to march stiffly along the east rampart, holding his musket over his shoulder muzzle down, clutching it by the bayonet. Two sober soldiers who came across three Dutch mercenaries ransacking Drake's bedroom had to flee for their lives when the Dutchmen, with screaming guttural oaths, chased them across the parade-ground with knives.

Leaving only a few officers to guard the walls, Holwell called all the Europeans to a war council. They all stood in the council chamber, afraid that if once they sat they would fall asleep. The magistrate offered arrack to any who wished, and told them that they must face the truth: they could not hold out much longer. But he beseeched them to remain at their posts until the following morning, insisting that the longer they held the Fort, the stronger would be his position for bargaining for their lives when the moment came to surrender.

Though there was little fighting after dark, it must have been a terrible night for the defenders. 'The enemy suspended their attack as usual when it grew dark,' said Cooke in his evidence, 'but the night was not less dreadful on that account. The Company's house, Mr Cruttenden's, Mr Nixon's and the marine yard were now in flames, and exhibited a spectacle of unspeakable horror. We were surrounded on all sides by the Nabob's forces, which made a retreat by land impracticable; and we had not even the shadow of a prospect to effect a retreat by water after the *Prince George* ran aground.'

All through that night the Nabob's plunderers were busily sacking what little was left of White Town. For the women who watched from the ships, whose husbands, fathers and sons had been betrayed, the sight must have been indescribably distressing. The fires were so widespread that none of them could decide if they came from the Fort itself or from the near-by houses; none could tell if fathers or brothers were alive or if the Nabob had taken the Fort. Perhaps at first they had hoped that the ships would return, until the flames in the night must have told them that it was too late.

One more shameful incident on that awful night has still to be recounted. It was nothing less than treachery and began when Hedleburgh, the Dutch sergeant (who had already been bribed by St Jacques), gathered together some fifty Dutch mercenaries and began to plot the act which was to lead to the final downfall of the Fort. Naturally we know little of this secret meeting, but in view of what happened the following day, it was certainly Hedleburgh who arranged for several of the

Dutchmen to escape during the night into the Indian lines.

His plan had been carefully laid in conjunction with the Indians. On the next day a Moorish officer would if possible approach the Fort, ostensibly to discuss the possibility of a truce. While the garrison was lulled into believing the fighting had ended, Hedleburgh would, at a given sign, force open the river-bank gate in the fence below the south-west bastion while his fellow conspirators, who had already made contact with the Nabob's forces, would lead his crack troops through the back gate and the colonnade into the Governor's residence. If it were not possible to stage a false truce—or if the garrison's leaders were suspicious of such an overture—then Hedleburgh would still try to force the gate, though the danger would be greater.

Not a soul in the Fort knew anything about this plan, which is not surprising when one considers the disorder and the vast number of refugees. All we know now is that, as midnight approached and half the garrison was asleep, Hedleburgh and two assistants crept silently up to the east curtain and strangled two guards near the east gate at a point just above the Black Hole arcade.

A few minutes later Hedleburgh stood there in the shadows and watched as fifty-six mercenaries, mostly Dutch, silently dropped over the walls into the dust of the south road. They were taken immediately to St Jacques, who was waiting for them in the church barely fifty yards away.

It was very dark that night, an intense blackness broken only by the fires and the occasional orange stab of flame as an enemy gun fired. In the darkness, while the garrison slept, Holwell walked across the parade-ground to the west bastion overlooking the river, lonely and possibly a little afraid of what the morning would bring. Far away the occasional lantern twinkled from the ghostlike ships that had deserted the Fort, but for the most part the night sky was pitch black, lit only by a glow of vivid scarlet from the burning buildings.

CHAPTER EIGHT

Besieged and Betrayed

Sunday, June 20

By dawn on Sunday—'the most fateful Sunday ever known in Calcutta'—much of the smoke from the burning houses had cleared away and for the first time since the previous afternoon Fort William was clearly visible from the decks of the *Dodaldy*. The crew could see figures moving about, even hear the occasional cry or shout as it carried across the water amid the first early reverberations of cannon-fire. As the news spread, a growing crowd of women and children emerged from their miserable cabins and, lining the decks, peered hopefully towards the shore as the first grey light of dawn turned swiftly into the shimmering heat-haze of another day.

The ships still lay where they had anchored the previous night, about a mile down-river; but though the Fort was visible, the distance was too great for small ships' boats to make the double journey to take off the garrison, which most believed had perished.

Now, however, the sight which met their eyes seemed to indicate that, despite their fears of the previous night, a miracle had taken place; Fort William was still holding out. The raging fires which everyone believed had come from the Fort must have come instead from the blackened shells of the houses, for the grey walls of the Fort, its parapets, buildings, the lofty magnificence of the

Governor's House, were still there, battered but defiant. They could plainly see the British flag flying like a token of hope.

The excitement, the wave of hope which this sight aroused in the crowd of women who now besieged Drake, Manningham and Captain Young, imploring them to return to take off their men, must have been pathetically heart-rending—for their pleas were met with blank refusal. Girls like Anna Bellamy could plainly see the enemy close under the south bastion, but though their relatives continued to send out signals demanding assistance, Drake and Young insisted that they were being hung out by the enemy to lure the vessels back; and so no notice was taken of them despite the women's pleas.

Incredible as it may seem, the men who had deserted, who had abandoned their companions in the Fort and even refused them the loan of a spare anchor now chose —and one can only assume the choice was calculated— to convince themselves that the signals from shore were decoys and that the Fort had fallen. Captain Young (who had the insolence later to put in a claim for minor damage to his vessel) had the last word, for he was master of the ship; but the part-owners of the *Dodaldy* and the Governor must share the blame for this inhuman self-deception.

William Mackett, whose wife's health had recovered a little that morning, was so horrified that he left her with Sarah Mapletoft in their cabin in the round-house and begged Drake to lend him a ship's boat and volunteer crew. He was convinced, he said, the distress signals were genuine, and suggested that it was only necessary to row half-way out from the *Dodaldy* towards the river bank in order to make certain. Once it had been established the Fort was still holding out, it would be a simple matter for the *Dodaldy* to move close in immediately and pick up the garrison.

To his horror, Drake and Young would have none of it. The signals, they maintained vehemently, were false and it was unthinkable to expose the women and children to the slightest risk. There was no point in argument.

More and more women crossed the crowded decks to the captain's cabin to support Mackett's pleas—any risk, they implored, would be worthwhile should there be a hope of rescuing their men. Drake and Young, however, remained adamant. The ladies, they coldly suggested, would be better occupied remaining below decks; war was a man's business. As for Mr Mackett (who was, after all, a senior member of the Council), it appears that they treated him with the scorn normally reserved for an impudent schoolboy.

Yet the danger involved in discovering the real situation on shore was negligible. As Holwell later stated to the Court of Directors, 'the danger of returning to the ships has, I hear, been alleged . . . it has been urged that they were at no certainty whether we were in possession of the Fort or not, and by some conjectured that we had surrendered or the place had been taken by assault, and that the flag was only kept by the enemy to decoy the fleet back. But if these were the doubts that actuated them, why did they not satisfy themselves? A single sloop or boat sent up . . . might have hailed us on the bastions without risk, even had the place been in possession of the enemy, the contrary of which they would have ascertained of, and the fleet might have moved up. This motion would have put fresh spirits in us and given dismay to the enemy . . . and a general retreat been made of the whole garrison, as glorious to ourselves, all circumstances considered, as a victory would have been; the gentlemen would have found a plan already formed, to the minutest circumstance, for a general retreat, that would have been attended with no disorder, confusion or difficulty.'

This was perfectly true. During the night Holwell and his senior officers had made careful preparations for an orderly retreat. They could hardly believe their good fortune when dawn had come and the masts of the ships were seen peeping above the morning mist; naturally they immediately concluded that, despite the events of the previous day, the ships had remained so that they could move in to pick them up. What else could they have thought?

Then, as reality slowly dawned, an almost unbearable anguish must have overtaken them as they realized the ships they could see at anchor remained brutally indifferent to their desperate signals for help. Even in those harsh days it must have been difficult to credit their late commanders and comrades with such callousness and it must have taken the garrison a long, long time to accept the almost unbelievable truth.

One of the curious circumstances to which history gives us no clue is why no other vessel attempted to rescue the garrison that morning. Besides the *Dodaldy*, there were several large ships unencumbered by women and children (and thus bereft of any convenient cloak for cowardice). Why did not a single captain decide to act on his own initiative? The average Indiaman was fitted out like a man-o'-war, their captains were used to taking risks during the long voyage from England, and were adept at repelling the most determined attacks. Yet there is no evidence that any vessel attempted to rescue the garrison.

Undoubtedly there was so much confusion that some captains may really not have grasped what was happening, nor was there any simple means of exchanging messages.

Even so, it seems strange. But the other vessels doubtless took their lead from the *Dodaldy*, knowing the settlement's leaders were on board, and Holwell was probably right in saying, 'had your President . . . on the *Dodaldy* . . . moved up even [on] the 20th, not a man or vessel but would have followed him.' But not a ship *did* move up—and the abandoned garrison was left with no alternative but to fight on or surrender.

No detailed accounts exist of the actual fighting on this last morning of the siege, though we are left in no doubt that it was fierce and intense. The garrison's losses,͵ however, were now mounting so swiftly that Holwell soon found himself faced with increasingly urgent demands to make an immediate surrender. So strong were these that when forty men in one bastion —mostly Portuguese and Armenian—were killed or wounded in a single engagement, even some of the officers joined in the growing clamour for a truce.

Holwell now had no alternative but to make a desperate decision. By mid-morning, twenty-five of the garrison had been killed and seventy wounded. All but fourteen of his gunners were also dead. Yet, 'though the enemy formed three assaults at once against the north-west bastion and against the windows on the east curtain', (i.e. the holes previously pierced there to let in air) Holwell's every instinct urged him to hold out as long as possible.

It was no question of false heroics, but a simple matter of logic. For Holwell, with all his experience of the Indians' psychology, was well aware that their commanders, furious over their heavy losses, would seize upon the slightest evidence of weakness—the slightest suspicion of unconditional surrender—as a pretext to inflict bloody vengeance on the remnants of the garrison before the Nabob could prevent them. The only hope of averting such vengeance lay in a personal approach to the Nabob in order to make him believe that a still formidable fighting force was now ready to surrender in the face of overwhelming superior power. Could such a mission be accomplished, there might still be some hope for the garrison in a country where the codes of war demanded that the more courage an enemy displayed, the more honourable must be the terms of peace. It was one thing, however, for Holwell to know what he ought to do; it was another to make the garrison understand the delay this would incur while all around men were constantly being killed or wounded in onslaughts that seemed to increase in fury as the hours went past.

It must have been shortly before noon when he was explaining to the officers in the council chamber what he intended to do that Lieutenant Witherington rushed in, gasping that the last of the powder had been used. 'There is no dry powder left,' he is recorded as announcing. 'Only a small amount that is wet.'

As Witherington blurted out the news, the officers and several civilians thronged around Holwell, begging him to hang out a flag of truce. Anything to save lives. All hope now seemed to have vanished.

Yet this remarkable man still hesitated. Turning on the miserable Lieutenant, he accused him of exaggerating. His questions were stern and to the point. Was Witherington sure he was right? How long ago had he visited the armoury and had a check been kept on the supplies already distributed? How could the Lieutenant be absolutely certain, Holwell demanded, that there was literally not a grain of dry powder left anywhere in the entire Fort?

Having reduced the unlucky man to stammering uncertainty, Holwell now turned to the crowded room. He demanded no miracles but just enough powder for an hour or two. If they could find that, he promised to surrender before nightfall.

And of course, incredible though it may seem to us, it turned out there *was* some powder; very little, it was true, but Holwell recorded that, when pressed, Witherington finally admitted there was sufficient for a few hours 'at the utmost'.

The weary officers and civilians, worn down by the strain thrust so unrelentingly upon them, now started shouting and arguing until Holwell held up his hands for silence and then, in simple direct language, explained why the fight must be continued. He would, he promised them, go immediately and force Omichand to write a letter to the Nabob, but only if the garrison trusted in him and promised to fight on until the Nabob sent an emissary to the Fort. If they would do this, they still had a chance. But he was convinced that the enemy must believe they could still withstand a siege. Once he had made the Nabob realize this, then he would throw out a flag of truce—with a much better prospect of success.

For a moment there was silence—the silence of doubt —in that hot, crowded council chamber where Drake had wasted so many futile hours and where the sun now blazed in through the hole made by the cannon-ball which had broken up the first midnight meeting.

Finally one officer shouted that he would fight on and almost immediately the others were shouting agreement too—Lushington, John Bellamy, Piccard and Carey. The confidence in Holwell was extraordinary, even though some may have entertained private fears. Yet they all seemed resolved to die if they had to in defence of their honour.

According to one legend, a lonely female voice joined in the chorus of approval. Unknown to anyone, Lady

Russell must have crept in from her hospital room next door to watch this historic meeting.

Assured of support, Holwell, accompanied by Lushington, now made his way across the parade-ground to visit Omichand in the Black Hole, struggling to force a passage through the crowded refugees, through misery and squalor, dirt and debris, that now seemed to choke that once vast and immaculate square.

The scene on the parade-ground was appalling. The physical miseries with which the defenders had to contend were overwhelming. The flies had been bad enough, but now the rats had emerged from the underground caverns in their hundreds. It was as though they sensed safety and licence now that the garrison was preoccupied with destruction elsewhere. They were so brazen that when an officer kicked two from a corpse they did not scurry away but waited for the men to pass and as they moved on they returned to their feast.

Since the coolies had long since fled and no soldiers could be spared to cart away the bodies, the corpses of numerous unfortunate natives, including women and children, lay where they had been killed by cannon-fire, often in the grotesque postures of sudden death. The stench was overpowering.

In one corner Lushington came across a scene bizarre almost beyond belief. Amid all the filth, the dead and the wounded, the flies and the rats, he discovered a rich Hindu refugee decorously eating a meal off a succession of spotless plates. The man was squatting on a coloured mat, two slaves hovering around to serve him, while the remainder of his numerous entourage formed themselves into a human square of privacy round him, apparently oblivious of all the misery and hunger and cries of their less fortunate neighbours.

But it was the Fort now rather than the refugees which worried Holwell. The damage was extensive. Whichever way one looked, one was aware of the damage caused by St Jacques's cannon. The roofs of Writers' Row yawned with ugly holes from the enemy's eighteen-pounder cannon-balls, while the ramparts—especially the east wall—displayed vast gashes as though some giant had sliced whole sections of the thin pucca walls away in sudden fury. Amid this devastation, the men along the parapets and on the bastions fired and reloaded as though motivated only by some inner mechanism which continued to function independently of their tired brains. The nightmarish quality of that last morning—where men fought, almost asleep as they stood, sustained only by a desperate longing for the midday cease-fire—has never been described for the simple reason that none of the survivors was later able to recall any details of the engagement.

It is not difficult to imagine Holwell's dismay at the sight of the robot-like figures on the ramparts; at the cannoneers at their posts amid this carnage and wreckage blindly, still automatically, carrying out the complicated gun drill, swilling down the hot barrels, reloading, ramming home the charges, preparing the portfires. Their appearance told him plainly that here were men who had reached and gone beyond the limit of endurance. No man had slept properly or washed for days. Their uniforms had long since been reduced to tattered remnants of scarlet jackets or shirts. Some fought stripped to the waist, and every so often a man would drop from sunstroke in the broiling heat.

The vaulted roof of the heavy stone arches contrived to deaden the noise a little as Holwell and Lushington hurried through the arcade towards the Black Hole, but when they reached the door of the prison, Holwell suddenly hesitated and ordered the guard to bring Omichand outside into the arcade.

As Omichand waddled out, even Holwell felt a moment's pity for the bedraggled, filthy object which now confronted him. Omichand had spent several days in gaol (and one can imagine the casual fashion in which he must have been fed). Now, the folds of his dewlaps hung loosely, his skin was grey beneath the dirt, his once-clean silk gown was filthy. Nevertheless, he retained some vestige of dignity and as he bowed ceremoniously to Holwell, his black eyes glittered with hate he could never control.

Holwell came to the point quickly. The garrison had sufficient food and powder to withstand a siege for an indefinite period. The ships were still lying in the Hoogly. Reinforcements would certainly arrive from Madras. In the meantime, both Indian and British casualties were heavy, and trade was at a standstill. But, as Holwell was careful to point out, the Nabob's quarrel had never really been with the British settlement, but with Drake; and Drake had now left Calcutta. He, Holwell, was Acting Governor. This being so, would it not be wiser for all concerned to avoid any more unnecessary bloodshed?

It was a masterly argument and Holwell apparently had no difficulty in persuading Omichand to write the vital letter to the Nabob, even though he made it plain that he would agree to a cease-fire only on the understanding that the garrison would be treated honourably.

Several historians have wondered why Omichand, who had refused to write to the Nabob at the beginning of the siege, now suddenly changed his mind. The reason surely lies in the fact that Omichand must have known of Hedleburgh's plot to betray the Fort. He may not have been implicated in the actual conspiracy, but it is extremely unlikely that he was ignorant of the plan afoot. Amid the confusion of the fighting, the drunkenness and lack of discipline, Hedleburgh could have had no difficulty in keeping Omichand informed. Messages could have been passed through the grilled windows of the Black Hole, or even whispered through them. For however incredible it may now seem, it is indisputable that even at the height of the fighting men were still able to walk anywhere they pleased or leave the Fort if they felt so inclined, especially during the night or the midday lull.

Holwell, with no suspicion of the plot, must have felt he had scored a diplomatic victory of the utmost significance. And Omichand, too, must have realized the instant Holwell came to see him that through writing the letter he would help the plotters. For now, if and when the Nabob's emissary should appear, the garrison would assume he came in response to Omichand's letter. If this happened, Hedleburgh's men would be able to force the river gate without any opposition from the defenders, who would naturally be under the impression that it was the Nabob who had offered them a truce.

This, in fact, is almost exactly what happened.

The drama was now swiftly approaching its climax. At noon all fighting ceased according to custom, and the weary defenders laid down their arms and either ate or—more likely—fell asleep wherever they happened to be.

Holwell and Gervas Bellamy walked over to the dining-hall in Writers' Row, where it was Mary Carey's turn to boil the rice for the meal. Both men made some pretence at eating but they had little stomach for food. The dining-room was a shambles. The walls gaped with holes, the long tables and the high-backed chairs—fashioned with such care—had been smashed and twisted and ripped until they looked like so much firewood. Only one long table remained untouched in the midst of the debris. A sullen Captain Clayton sat alone. Carey was sitting at one end with Piccard and Leach, and soon they were joined by several of the younger officers. While everybody was eating, a curious incident occurred. It was some hours before Holwell was to realize its significance.

Leach was the sort of loyal, hard-working carpenter we would today describe as 'one of the old school'; he had always admired Holwell and now he walked up to where he sat and began to whisper in his ear. We do not know his precise words, but in a rambling, nervous way he said in effect that the Zemindar had no need to worry, if the worst came to the worst Leach knew a secret escape passage out of the Fort.

Holwell, dead tired and desperately worried, probably wondered what on earth the man was babbling on about, but before he had time to make even a non-committal reply, John Bellamy rushed in crying that one of the Nabob's officers was approaching the east gate along The Avenue, making signs to the sentries not to fire.

Filled with a sudden surge of excitement, Holwell jumped up. It was just two o'clock.

All the occupants of the dining-hall followed him as he strode across the parade-ground, pushing through the refugee children begging for food and water. He climbed the stone steps leading to the south-east bastion so quickly that the others had difficulty in keeping up with him. He could hardly wait to reach the ramparts. Poor Holwell! Little suspecting what had happened—or what was about to happen—one can imagine the unanswered questions in his mind. He had hardly dared hope for such a swift reply to Omichand's letter. Now, the only thing that mattered was to save the lives of the garrison.

As he peered over the ramparts, Holwell could see
that the emissary appeared to be a high-ranking officer.
He was dressed in a uniform of sorts, carried a sabre,
and wore a turban of the Nabob's royal indigo; he was
alone. It must have been a moment of uncanny drama.
All noise of battle had died down and now the east wall
of the Fort became suddenly crowded with anxious
officers and men, leaning over the parapets waiting and
watching as the lone figure slowly approached along the
empty street.

There was no sign of the enemy. The church must
have been crammed with Indian troops, yet now it was
so silent one might have believed it empty. The jagged
and blackened ruins of Calcutta's greatest houses framed
the other side of the dusty street, which was littered with
smashed-up gun-carriages, wrecked cannon, carcasses of
horses and bullocks rotting in the sun, even a few human
corpses. Still the emissary strode on, apparently uncon-
cerned at the desolation around him.

When the man was twenty yards away, Holwell
climbed on the parapet wall and hailed him. The envoy
stopped. Holwell held up a hand and the man returned
the greeting in reasonably good English and with a polite
salaam. When Holwell asked him the purpose of his
visit, the envoy replied that he came with a message from
his master the Nabob 'that if the fighting ceased an
accommodation might be come to'.

Holwell had no reason to doubt that the emissary was
there as a result of Omichand's letter and agreed to
order a cease-fire, insisting, however, that he must have
the Nabob's promise to treat the garrison honourably.
To this the envoy replied that he would return to his
master and deliver this message. Meanwhile, they had
his master's word that all fighting would stop until the
Nabob's pleasure was known.

We shall never know whether this envoy did in fact come from the Nabob, or whether his appearance was part of Hedleburgh's deep-laid plot. For the Nabob, however cruel and vicious, lived according to a peculiar code of honour of his own, and it is hard to believe he would have given his word to cease fighting in the full knowledge that the pledge would shortly be broken. It seems more likely that Omichand's letter—which had been so fortuitously requested—never reached the Nabob. Probably it had been mislaid, the plotters well aware that once Holwell believed the Nabob had received it, the sudden appearance of an envoy would seem natural and plausible since nobody would doubt the honest intentions of the truce.

In a matter of moments the brief ceremony was over. As Holwell turned and ordered Carey to hoist a flag of truce, a tremendous cheer broke out along the battlements and the exhausted but deliriously relieved garrison watched the envoy make his farewell salaam to Holwell, then turn without another word and walk slowly and deliberately up The Avenue towards the cross-roads.

Holwell now held up his hand for silence and as the cheering subsided, told the men to 'lay down your arms, rest and refresh yourselves'.

The long-awaited truce was now reality; it must have been a moment of supreme pride for Holwell—and a moment of shattering emotion for the ordinary soldiers who doubtless regarded it as the end to all fighting. The news swept round the Fort in minutes. Lady Russell was in the hospital, where several men she had believed on the point of death recovered with miraculous rapidity and cheered till they could cheer no more. Mary Carey was laughing as she doled out double portions of rice and hot flat chapattis to Blagg, Lushington and the other youngsters, who, now the tension was gone, instinctively made for the dining-hall.

Most of them were too excited to rest as Holwell had advised them, for it was easy for the youngsters to imagine that at long last the siege and the danger were over; but as for Holwell, he went to the headquarters he had established in Drake's mansion and split a bottle of claret with the old chaplain. Though hopeful, he remained uneasy, still doubting in his mind whether the news was not too good to be true. Even later he was never able to explain the reason for this instinctive suspicion. One supposes that, as a good doctor (and an equally good lawyer), he automatically distrusted good news which arrived too easily.

Henry Lushington, in his role as aide, apparently left the others in Writers' Row to see if he could be of service to Holwell (who, unlike Drake, invariably left precise details of his whereabouts). The magistrate and the chaplain both appeared very fatigued, but Holwell offered him a glass, which he refused. However, Lushington, who was only eighteen, must have been a fine young man, for he decided to remain within call in case his presence was needed.

So the two men—Holwell aged forty-five and the chaplain aged sixty-five—lived through the brief moments of betrayed hope alone in the room where Drake had once lived. They must have had a couple of glasses of claret, no more, then fallen asleep where they sat, for that is how Lushington found them when his presence was needed, asleep at the table, each with his head cradled in his arms.

It had been agreed the truce should last until the envoy returned to make known the Nabob's terms. And at first all seemed to go well. In Bengal (and for that matter anywhere else in the eighteenth century) time was not the same precious currency we know today. The hours of waiting which now ensued aroused no alarm since nobody expected an immediate reply. In any case it was now the hour of siesta, and it was well-known that not even the most trusted adviser would dare to awaken the Nabob.

Three o'clock came and went and the silence in the hot, still air of the Calcutta afternoon seemed so strange after the clamour and exhaustion of the recent fighting that the members of the garrison began to react in an uncharacteristic way. Perhaps the long-drawn strain was now exacting its toll, for we know that men ignored Holwell's wise advice to rest. Soldiers and civilians who earlier that day had been fighting in a stupor of exhaustion now started sprucing up their tattered uniforms. Two soldiers were observed clearing up the shambles of the south-east bastion. Men at the other bastions, jealous of these attempts, started to emulate—even to better— them. One soldier began polishing the barrel of a brass field-piece. Another was seen sweeping the arcade. Men hastened to volunteer for all kinds of unnecessary duties. Somehow one imagines their tired minds had understood that when the truce was finalized, the Nabob would enter Fort William in triumph, and it was as though each man was determined to look his best for the occasion and in his own manner flaunt his pride in the impregnable grey mass of the Fort which still stood, albeit battered and bruised, as a symbol of the bravery, if not the might, of the British in India.

At four o'clock the illusion was shattered.

One moment The Avenue appeared empty and quiet. The next, as though at some pre-arranged signal, thousands of the Nabob's men started pouring out of the compounds, the big houses, and the church. John Bellamy and Piccard were on the east wall. In an instant —almost before they had time to send a messenger rushing to find Holwell—the enemy was crowding close up to the walls, yelling and screaming. No shots were fired for the moment, but the crowd of soldiers had a most menacing appearance as Holwell ran along the east wall to join Bellamy and Piccard. Several officers trained their muskets on the crowd, but Holwell shouted to them to hold their fire, unable to believe that some ghastly mistake had not occurred.

An officer named Baillie was standing next to Holwell as the magistrate appealed to the crowd below—and restrained his own men. Suddenly a musket-shot sang out from The Avenue and Baillie dropped to the ground, blood spurting from a superficial wound in his head. The shot had obviously been intended for Holwell, and now the garrison began firing wildly as the Indians tried to rush the east gate. The men on the ramparts did not know—could not guess—that even this was only a feint attack to draw the defenders away from the river as the moment of treachery approached.

Almost the whole garrison seemed to have crowded on to the east wall, firing down on the crowd, using up their last grains of powder, when Leach, who had been stationed on the south-west bastion overlooking the river, observed a sight which made him gasp with horror. In an instant he was running across the parade-ground calling loudly for help.

Unsuspected by the garrison, the fifty-six Dutch deserters, strengthened by a detachment of picked enemy troops, had been hiding in the burned-out shell of the Company House during the siesta. Now—as the carefully planned diversion at the east gate was attracting the defenders' attention—Sergeant Hedleburgh crept down through the Governor's colonnade and darted across the mud-flats towards the fence running from the south-west bastion to the river bank. Leach was the only man on the bastion—and he had no powder left. He ran for help. It was all he could do.

The gate in this vital fence had been secured with old-fashioned locks and bolts but Hedleburgh was a man of prodigious strength. Grunting and sweating, he wrenched at the bolts with his bare hands. It was a remarkable feat, even though the woodwork was probably rotten and half eaten away.

As soon as Leach, breathless and gasping, had brought this news to the east curtain, Lieutenant Blagg and Ensign Piccard with six men dashed across the parade-ground in a desperate effort to avert disaster. Before they could reach the Governor's House, however, Hedleburgh had torn off the locks and the deserters came pouring through, led by the Dutch sergeant—a yelling, triumphant, half-drunken mob—through the colonnade and into the Governor's mansion.

The mob of soldiers reached the riverside entrance to the mansion almost exactly at the moment Blagg and Piccard dashed in by the parade-ground entrance and the two forces clashed head-on in the corridor near the hospital room. With hardly any powder left, the defenders never stood a chance. Every man was cut down. Here Piccard, who had fought so magnificently at Perrin's Redoubt, was the first to fall as the first wave engulfed him; here, the young and gallant Lieutenant Blagg refused to lay down his sword and fought to the last before he too was cut down. In a few seconds the mob was trampling over their dead bodies and swarming on to the parade-ground.

Every one of the defenders now prepared to die fighting, for no mercy could be expected from the Nabob, and as the Dutch started milling on to the parade-ground, attacking any English whom they encountered, a strong body of native troops began scaling the east wall by means of bamboos which they used as ladders. The garrison there rushed to repel them, but overwhelmed by ever-increasing numbers, went down fighting. 'All who resisted, especially those who still wore scarlet coats, were mercilessly cut to pieces' as more and more of the enemy climbed over the east wall, while others along the bank of the Hoogly poured in in increasing numbers through the river gate.

Meanwhile, what had happened to Holwell? The instant Baillie was hit, it seems, he dashed up to the south-east bastion and had a cannon trained on the crowd below, shouting to them that he would fire instantly if they did not disperse. He then ran down from the bastion to the parade-ground, where he ordered 'a general discharge of cannon and small-arms'. He had yet to learn what had happened to Blagg and Piccard, but at this moment two officers 'came running to me and told me the western [river] gate was forced by our own people and betrayed . . . the locks and bolts were forced off.'

Worse was to follow. Holwell stumbled back to the south-east bastion and had almost reached the top of the steps leading from the parade-ground, when he saw to his horror the Nabob's colours being suddenly hoisted on the river bastion behind the Governor's House. Obviously the mob surging through the river gate had overwhelmed the bastion by attacking it from the parade-ground. Utterly dismayed, Holwell paused on the steps, 'and turning myself I saw below multitudes of the enemy who had entered that way [the river gate] and others who had scaled by the south-west bastion and the new godowns [warehouses] deserted at the time the gate was forced.'

What happened next is not entirely clear, for the survivors' chronicles and the evidence at the enquiry later seem to ignore details of the final fighting. It seems hard to believe that it suddenly ceased abruptly at this point, yet several brave officers and men, Bellamy, Lushington and Carey among them, who might have been expected to meet the same fate as Blagg and Piccard, were not killed or wounded despite the enemy now flooding into the Fort, and all we really know for certain is outlined in Holwell's narrative. 'To the first jemmautdaar [officer] who scaled at the south-west bastion I advanced and delivered my pistols.'

The Nabob's officer then curtly told the magistrate to order the British colours to be cut down immediately.

Holwell must have been mortified beyond belief at this unexpected turn of events and horrified that this plan for saving the garrison had gone awry; but he flatly refused to obey the officer. 'I replied I would give no such orders, they were masters of the Fort and might order it themselves.'

The officer then ordered Holwell to give up his sword —and again Holwell stood his ground. 'I refused delivering it but in the presence of the Suba [Nabob].'

Now it was all over. The Fort was betrayed and captured, and as the fighting ceased, despondent groups of men, filled with fears and anxieties, stood in knots on the parade-ground or in the arcade, waiting to see what would happen to them, standing there rigid and angry as the Moors tore off the buckles from men's shoes and the buttons from their coats.

The Indians looted the Fort in ruthless and systematic fashion, but did not harm any of the garrison. Indeed, their control over the prisoners was so lax that several men escaped merely by walking out of the river gate and making their way to Surman's Gardens, south of Calcutta, where they were later picked up by the ships. Among their numbers was the redoubtable Lady Russell, who at first had refused to leave until a native officer had announced that all the Portuguese, Armenians and native prisoners could go free, on hearing which she knew no harm could come to Mary Carey.

Lady Russell now begged Mary to escape with her, but this brave girl insisted on staying. Her husband Peter was now a prisoner, and though she herself was free, she preferred to stay in order to see what happened to him. Holwell, who was anxious for Lady Russell's safety, persuaded Leach to accompany her, and finally this remarkable woman, who had played such a magnificent role throughout the siege, made the last rounds of the tiny hospital she had virtually created, saw her patients were comfortable, and prepared to leave.

She and Leach crept through the river gate and slushed ankle-deep in the mud of the river bank, which was crowded with milling men and women, British as well as natives, trying to escape. In the vain hope of swimming to the ships some plunged into the river, where most were drowned. Others made for the jungle south of Holwell's house—some to perish when attacked by plunderers, others to reach Surman's Gardens and safety. Lady Russell and Leach were able to gain the comparative safety of the Company House and vanished inside its charred skeleton. It was the last sight anybody in the Fort had of the indomitable Lady Russell.

The Nabob's senior officer, who seemed to have taken no offence at Holwell's refusal to deliver up his sword, now returned to seek out the magistrate. He found Holwell standing by the foot of the steps on the parade-ground talking to Gervas Bellamy. Each had been stripped of every item of metal. The officer announced that the Nabob was arriving outside the east gate, and Holwell was taken to the ramparts so that he could see him. Standing on the parapet above the east gate, the enemy officer made a signal to stop, then he prostrated himself. Holwell stood at attention and looked over the top of the parapet on The Avenue. He could see the Nabob peering out of the litter in which he was sitting. Now that he was in the presence of his enemy, Holwell made the customary salaam and only then delivered his sword to the officer. The Nabob from his litter returned his salaam. After this Holwell was permitted to return to his colleagues on the parade-ground to await the Nabob's triumphant entry into Fort William.

The small group of Englishmen endured the moments before his arrival with a strange mixture of emotions in which one gathers that wounded pride dominated any feeling of apprehension. Nobody suspected the disaster that was about to overtake them, for hardly a man had been badly treated, except for having the buttons and badges stripped from their uniforms, and everybody could see that the officer dealing with Holwell behaved with scrupulous courtesy. Moreover, the half-castes were already pardoned and freed, the few remaining natives were streaming out to pick up what threads of their wretched lives they could find in the desolate desert of Black Town. Why then (so the men must have argued among themselves) should they have anything to fear? They had fought well, they had requested an honourable truce. They would now receive honourable treatment.

They were, however, reckoning without several factors. The calamitous losses inflicted on the Nabob's army might not have unduly concerned the Nabob, but they had without doubt enraged his commanders such

as Roy Doolub and St Jacques, who were now anxious
for revenge. Though the Nabob himself was savagely
cruel, he obeyed the etiquette and codes of war strictly.
What was to follow was not the result of his deliberate
cruelty, but sprang from a complete indifference to
suffering; the sort of indifference that made the Nabob's
troops unthinkingly regard a wounded comrade as a
cumbersome burden best left to die.

But most of all, the defenders must have reckoned
without the one cruel factor that had dogged them as
remorselessly as the Nabob's troops—bad luck. For once
again it was bad luck more than anything else that was,
within the space of two hours, to extinguish their hopes
and cost most of them their lives.

The Nabob made his entry into Fort William by the
small river gate opposite the flagstaff.

It was an unexpected choice, but apparently he desired
to make a tour of the outside walls before making a
triumphant entry. The south road and The Avenue were
crammed with cheering troops, and the Nabob was
carried in a splendid litter by six men. Roy Doolub, St
Jacques and many other senior officers followed on horseback or on foot. The procession turned left at the north-
west bastion and the Nabob was slowly carried the three
hundred feet to the river bank, where he could plainly
see the black hulk of the *Prince George*. The gate in the
northern river fence had of course been opened for him,
and the Nabob with his magnificently attired retinue was
carried up the steps into the Fort, and his litter was set
down in the open space behind Writers' Row.

The grand entrance was marked with colourful ceremony. Hundreds of his personal bodyguard, recogniz-
able by their indigo *dhotis* and turbans, had preceded him

and now lined his route, keeping the curious natives and the few Englishmen at a distance. They must have behaved similarly to the British police on a state occasion, for the Nabob was one of the world's great rulers, and a stickler for ceremony and protocol.

It was protocol that caused the Nabob to receive first his relative Kissendass, who had pride of place because of his royal blood. After Kissendass (who must have been more than worried) had made his salaams, the Nabob presented this man—who had been one of the root causes of the siege—with a ceremonial dress; a sign that all was forgiven. (Some historians suggest that the Nabob's gift implied that he had sent Kissendass to Calcutta as a ruse, in order to provide a suitable excuse to attack the city!)

Kissendass departed, and next Omichand was ushered before the Nabob. The obese merchant had somehow contrived to acquire a clean robe and had spruced himself up for the occasion. Though not honoured with a ceremonial dress, there can be no doubt that the Nabob's reward consisted of promises well suited to Omichand's greed and desire for wealth.

The Nabob was now carried through the alley in Writers' Row and into the southern section of the Fort, which was also lined with hundreds of his bodyguards. He toured it extensively, making a thorough inspection of Drake's house, before deigning to speak to the British.

It was on the parade-ground that he summoned Holwell before him and this momentous scene is easy to re-create. One can visualize the pomp and splendour of the Nabob's retinue, the languid figure of this young and cruel potentate reclining in his ornate palanquin, the hundreds of troops in indigo-coloured garments crowded on the parade-ground and looking down from the ramparts, the thousands of pennants, listless in the warm, sultry dusk. It is not difficult either to imagine the sullen faces of the vanquished, peering as best they could through the serried ranks of armed guards.

When Holwell was brought before the Nabob on this first occasion, it was observed that his hands had been tied, but the Nabob angrily ordered his bonds to be cut.

Courtesies may have been observed, but the Nabob was an angry man. 'He expressed much resentment at our presumption in defending the Fort against his army with so few men,' wrote Holwell. The Nabob hardly moved as Holwell stood before him; his black, hard eyes watched him unblinkingly as he shot question after question at him. Why had he not fled with the Governor, he asked—but before Holwell had time to reply, where was the treasure? 'He seemed much disappointed and dissatisfied at the sum found in the Treasury, asked me many questions on this subject.'

Holwell stood his ground, making the best replies he could, but he could not tell where the treasure was because he did not know. One thing only was dominant in his mind—the necessity for obtaining honourable terms for his men. But it was difficult to broach the subject because for a long time the Nabob complained bitterly about the lack of treasure.

How Holwell contrived it we have no means of knowing, but in the end he was able to extract categorical promises that the Europeans would be well treated. And indeed, he stated later, 'on the conclusion he [the Nabob] assured me, on the word of a soldier, that no harm should come to me, which he repeated more than once.'

The Nabob followed up this promise with another tirade against Drake, and terminated the interview with a curt order to one of his generals to burn down the whole of Drake's splendid residence, under the mistaken impression that it belonged to Drake personally.

The first flames were already licking their way up the walls of Drake's mansion as Holwell returned to his men. Despite some reservations, he must have been relieved by the promises he had extracted, and there seemed no reason to suspect they would not be kept. They had been made in the presence of senior officers; indeed, when he returned to the arcade with the news, which was received with jubilation, a senior officer accompanied him and ordered the guards to allow the British reasonable freedom.

Yet, as the Nabob left the Fort the prisoners' hopes must have been tinged with apprehension, for by now all Fort William seemed to be ablaze. The Governor's residence 'was in flames to the right and left of us'. The armoury and the laboratory on the other side of Writers' Row were burning. So was the carpenters' yard.

Holwell tells how, as soon as it was dark, 'we were all, without distinction, directed by the guard over us to collect ourselves in one body and sit down quietly under the arched verandah or piazza' near the Black Hole prison, while in front of them on the parade-ground 'about four and five hundred gunmen with lighted matches' were drawn up in formation. 'The fire advanced with rapidity on both sides,' recalled Holwell, 'and it was the prevailing opinion that they intended suffocating us between the two fires; and this notion was confirmed by the appearance, about half an hour past seven, of some officers and people, with lighted torches in their hands.'

The prisoners' immediate reaction was a suspicion that the new troops were about to start more fires 'to expedite their scheme of burning us', and in desperation, the survivors saw no alternative but to rush the guard,

seize their scimitars and attack the troops on the parade-
ground, 'rather than be thus tamely roasted to death'.

One can imagine the younger officers devising these
desperate plans of escape, but Holwell's wiser counsels
calmed them, especially when he insisted on going himself to see if the officers with the torches, who had so
suddenly appeared, were in fact setting fire to buildings.
It was just as well he insisted on doing this, for it turned
out that they were merely examining the inner 'half-
rooms' in the arcade to see if they were large enough to
house the prisoners for the night.

The emotions of the prisoners at this time seem to have
fluctuated between hope and despair. At one moment
they were despondent, thinking the worst—that they
would be roasted alive. The next, when Holwell told
them all was well, their spirits soared, and they even
started making plans for the future.

It was now that Holwell was suddenly astonished to
see a figure standing in front of him—of all men it was
Leach the carpenter, who had last been seen escaping
with Lady Russell. Leach drew him aside. Lady Russell,
he reported, was well on her way by now to Surman's
Gardens and safety; she had met up with some escapers
who were helping her; Leach, however, had decided to
return.

Looking at the flames around them slowly creeping
nearer, Holwell must have thought him mad; but then,
to his further astonishment, Leach reminded the magistrate of their earlier conversation, which he had completely forgotten. He had returned, he said, for the
express purpose of leading the magistrate to safety. He
explained that a secret passage existed under the Fort
leading straight to the banks of the Hoogly. There was
a boat hidden there—a budgerow large enough for two.
He now suggested that he and Holwell should creep

quietly across the parade-ground. Leach would lead the way to the boat and they could escape before anybody realized what had happened.

It must have been a temptation for the magistrate, for despite any hopes he entertained for his fellow prisoners' safety, he was aware of the Nabob's displeasure where he personally was concerned. Should the Nabob remain convinced that Holwell had hidden the elusive treasure— and he would take a lot of persuading to be convinced of the contrary—he might well be in danger of experiencing some of the Nabob's refinements of torture.

Holwell recounts the offer in some detail, describing Leach as 'a man to whom I had in many instances been a friend, and who, on this occasion, demonstrated his sensibility of it in a degree worthy of a much higher rank'. Almost wistfully he admits that any escape 'might easily have been accomplished, as the guard put over us took but very slight notice of us.' Yet he felt himself unable to desert the others. He thanked Leach but told him 'it was a step I could not prevail on myself to take, as I should thereby very ill repay the attachment the gentlemen of the garrison had shown to me; and that I was resolved to share their fate, be what it would.' He then pressed Leach to make his own escape while the chance remained. The boat was there, the guard was slack, and he could leave immediately. Leach, however, gallantly replied 'that he was resolved to share mine [fate] and would not leave me'.

Hardly was their conversation at an end when the guards drawn up on the parade-ground came over to them and the officers who had been searching the arcades ordered the prisoners under the inner line of arches into the cross-walled 'open' rooms which served as barracks for troops awaiting their turn of duty.

Again the spirits and hopes of the survivors soared,

for as Holwell recounted, 'the barracks, you may remember, have a large wooden platform for the soldiers to sleep on, and are open to the west [i.e. facing the parade-ground and Governor's House] by arches and a small parapet wall corresponding to the arches of the verandah without. In we went most readily and were pleasing ourselves with the prospect of passing a comfortable night on the platform, little dreaming of the infernal apartment in reserve for us.'

Some accounts record how the men laughed and joked; Gervas Bellamy and one or two senior members were actually overheard discussing the chances of Holwell being able to persuade the Nabob to order an immediate resumption of trade and commerce. Mary Carey, the only woman left in the Fort, must have been among them with her husband Peter. Not a man could have remotely visualized what was to happen next.

From across the parade-ground Moslem priests could be heard intoning complicated songs of thanksgiving. As John Cooke said in his testimony, 'as we had been left unmolested in our persons so long, our apprehensions of ill-usage and barbarity began to vanish; and we even entertained hopes not only of getting our liberty but of being suffered to re-establish our affairs and carry on our business . . . but these hopes and expectations very soon changed into as great a reverse as human creatures ever felt.'

The change came with appalling swiftness. At one moment every man was filled with high hopes, then suddenly a fight started not far away; a musket-shot cracked into the night, and as the men jumped up to see what was happening, one of the Nabob's soldiers slumped to the ground. The whole thing was a paltry affair. One of Hedleburgh's drunken Dutchmen had picked a quarrel with a native soldier. The British were not even near the shooting. But the death of one man in a drunken brawl was to have terrible consequences.

There seems little doubt that the Nabob's officers who saw the incident were well aware the prisoners had nothing to do with it. But it is equally certain that these same officers were anxious for an opportunity to avenge their heavy losses, and so far had been restrained only by the strict orders of the Nabob himself. Now the opportunity had unexpectedly arrived. An officer ran to break the news to Roy Doolub. Doubtless he exaggerated it, for Roy Doolub immediately went to see the Nabob, only to find him weary after the long day and irritable at being interrupted on so trivial a matter; Roy Doolub, however, insisted it was dangerous to leave the large body of English prisoners in comparative freedom. According to Hill in *Bengal 1756-57*, the Nabob 'asked where the Europeans were accustomed to confine soldiers who had misbehaved in any way. He was told in the Black Hole, and as some of his officers suggested it would be dangerous to leave so many prisoners at large during the night, he ordered that they should all be confined in it.'

The conception of the tragedy was as simple as that. Nor was there any truth in the legend which has grown up that the Nabob suffocated the prisoners out of a perverted sense of cruelty. One has no hesitation in accepting Cooke's testimony, the official text of which reads: 'the witness further said that he did not believe the Nabob had any intention of a massacre when he confined the English in the Black Hole; but that his intention was merely to confine them for the night, without knowing [whether] the prison was great or small.'

The senior officers, however, had but recently inspected the Black Hole, and when the order came there could never have been the slightest doubt in their minds as to what they were about to do. Without hesitation they

ordered the guards to cover the prisoners with their
muskets, and then, according to Holwell, 'ordered us to
go into the room . . . commonly called the Black Hole
prison . . . whilst others with clubs and drawn scimitars
pressed upon those of us next to them'.

There may have been some scuffling, some minor
resistance as the dismayed and terrified prisoners realized
instantly that something terrible was about to happen.
The enemy soldiers pushed at them ruthlessly. No
allowance was made for the twelve wounded officers
among them who were shoved, crawling and moaning,
to the doorway near the far end of the arcade. Yet perhaps a few still cannot have realized what was going to
happen, for, as Cooke said, 'while we were wondering
what this should mean and laughing at the oddity of it, a
party of fellows came and ordered us to walk into the
place before mentioned called the Black Hole.'

Holwell instantly realized the peril, for he knew the
Black Hole. But few of the prisoners, with the possible
exception of some of the soldiers, were familiar with its
size. Besides, it must have happened so swiftly; with so
little warning. There was no time to tell men they were
going to certain death, no voice to cry that it would have
been better to rush the guard, however hopeless the
attempt, 'and been', as one report says, 'as the lesser evil,
by our own choice cut to pieces'.

There was no time at all. Savagely the Moors pushed
and shoved at the hesitant crowd of men. 'This stroke',
Holwell added, 'was so sudden, so unexpected and the
throng and pressure so great upon us next the door of
the Black Hole prison, there was no resisting it; but like
one agitated wave impelling another, we were obliged
to give way and enter; the rest followed like a torrent.'

The magistrate was the first to be pushed through the
door into the dark room.

It was eighteen feet long and fourteen feet ten inches wide. Only two holes, barricaded with iron bars, admitted air from the dark, vaulted arcade still red with the reflected glow of the fires outside. Somehow, like figures in a Dantesque nightmare, the stumbling, dazed men and one woman were crushed inside one after the other through the single door, pushed sprawling on top of one another, fighting for space, for a foothold, some standing, some—the more fortunate—trampled to death in those first moments of the long night that lay ahead. When the door was finally locked on them, 145 men, including twelve wounded officers, and one woman, Mary Carey, had been forcibly thrust and crammed into the prison.

It was just eight o'clock on Sunday evening.

CHAPTER NINE

The Night of the Black Hole

Sunday, June 20, 8.0 p.m.—Monday, June 21, 6.0 a.m.

Holwell's account of the night in the Black Hole is a cry of despair. Yet it was written during the voyage home to England, nine months after the event, and nobody was more surprised than he at the stir it eventually caused, for as he said later: 'It appears in some places a little passionate; in other somewhat diffuse.'

It was a personal letter, never intended for publication, and it is precisely because it was written to 'a friend in whom the greatest confidence was placed' that it is fascinating. If one compares the accounts of the siege which Holwell wrote for the East India Company with this letter, one might be forgiven for thinking they were written by different men. The accounts are sober, carefully analysed and annotated—each paragraph numbered for reference—and reveal a highly trained legal mind, behind which Holwell's personal emotions are studiously concealed among the mass of facts and arguments marshalled to explain the downfall of the Fort. The facts are accurate, the judgments are cogent; yet the result might have come straight from the impersonal interior of a computer for all the emotion it betrays.

But the Black Hole letter is totally different, for here Holwell is plainly deeply and inextricably re-experiencing the dreadful Calvary of that terrible night. It is the man who writes rather than the lawyer, and one has only to turn the pages for the reason for all Holwell's previous actions to be made abundantly clear. Here, unwittingly portrayed, is the real man: that subtle compound of courage, fear, anguish, compassion, even suicidal tendencies; in short, a human being who, as contradictory as most of us, ached one moment for the calm peace of death, yet the next, with a sudden surge of spirit, was determined to live. It is as though Holwell, weary of the legalistic arguments which had been dragging on in Madras for months, had now sat down in the peace and solitude of his cabin as his small sloop ploughed across the Indian Ocean and finally unburdened himself, giving way to the emotions he has been desperately striving to hide for so long. The result is not only a document of historical importance, but one which provides a fascinating insight into his character.

Holwell was the first man to be thrust through the narrow doorway. Impelled more perhaps by instinct than by the weight of bodies and the flailing arms behind him, he stumbled towards the nearest window and grasped an iron bar. The officers seem to have been forced in next behind him, for almost at the same moment Clayton, Witherington and Baillie (who had been wounded in the head during the last moments of the siege) were followed by Lushington, Cooke (the Company Secretary) and Captain Mills, a volunteer from the *Diligence*, one of the ships. Carey was next, pushed across the room by the surge of humanity behind him. Holwell saw him grip Mary's waist to shield her; then they seemed to vanish in the semi-darkness as wave after wave of sweating, dirty, tired and tattered men were funnelled, stumbling, through the doorway and spilled into the room, scrambling over those who had fallen and were already being trampled to death in a mad, instinctive rush towards the only source of air—the two small windows.

Except for Holwell and one or two soldiers, not one of the prisoners had ever been into the room. Had they been at all familiar with its cramped space, its foul smell and lack of air, there could hardly have been a man who would not have fought to the death outside the door. But not one of them suspected the awful truth. More-over, it was dark except for the glare when the fires burned fiercely, and this moment had come on them with such startling suddenness that there was no time for thought. Like sheep they followed one another, pushed and prodded by the butts and swords from behind. Hol-well caught a glimpse of the chaplain's frightened face as he was violently shoved into the room. As the old man fell, his son John pulled him to his feet. Holwell shouted to them—but his words went unheard in the fearful din and confusion, and the last he saw of them at that time was the old chaplain being swept into the far corner of the room where they seemed to become lost in the shadows.

Outside the tiny barred windows, the Governor's House was a mass of flames. Inside, in those first chaotic moments, the men who could not get near the windows were pushed to the back of the room. Some climbed on to a platform which had originally been built for im-prisoned drunken soldiers to sleep on. Over six feet wide, it ran the length of the eighteen-foot room and was raised about four feet above the smooth plastered floor. Others, seeking to escape the mounting pressure from behind, scrambled underneath the platform, thinking they would be safer there—whereas in fact they were virtually imprisoned by those who were pushed in afterwards and jammed against the platform.

There was now pandemonium. Of the hundred and forty-six people crammed into the room, some twenty or thirty had probably climbed on to the platform while a similar number had found illusory sanctuary beneath it. Though Holwell does not describe the first moments in any detail, there can be little doubt that many of those who were pushed in first to make room for the final victims now being herded in were already being crushed or trampled to death, but in those first awful moments it must have been impossible to grasp exactly what was happening.

Another extraordinary fact has to be taken into account. Since the door of the Hole opened inwards, a considerable space must have been taken up by the arc of the open door as the last prisoner was squeezed into the room, thus making the crush inside even more unbearable. What is more, the fact that it opened inwards explains why it was never possible, once it was closed, for the massed weight of the prisoners to break it down. 'Many unsuccessful attempts were made to force the door,' wrote Holwell, 'but having nothing but our hands to work with, and the door opening inward, all endeavours were vain and fruitless.'

It is difficult to conceive of the terror of those first dreadful minutes as the last prisoners were forced in, blinded by the gloom; stumbling, desperately forcing their way into the press of those inside—already beginning to be seized by claustrophobic terror, fighting and struggling to keep a foothold, battling to stand upright with arms and shoulders pinioned; to breathe, to ensure life in a nightmare where every sweating, helpless neighbour crushed against them instinctively became an enemy.

It was difficult enough to breathe. The stench of the place was so bad that men vomited uncontrollably over their neighbours. And now the silent, tortured fight for air, for an extra inch of space, began. It was a relentless struggle, for every man who collapsed made more space for those who could still stand. The second a man sagged for want of air he was inevitably trampled to death.

From underneath the long platform came the moans of men rapidly suffocating to death. In their last frenzy some took out their pocket-knives and slashed at the unfortunate legs—each like a prison bar—of their companions who had been pushed against the platform and now unwittingly starved them of air. But it made no difference. The unfortunates whose flesh and veins were being lacerated were unable to move a finger to defend themselves, let alone give their demented comrades the air they craved, so great was the pressure from all sides.

The comradeship which had sprung up during the siege, the discipline, humanity, even the last innate shreds of decency, must have vanished as animal instincts came nakedly uppermost in this appalling fight for survival. As Holwell recorded, 'I saw every one giving way to the violence of passions, which I saw must be fatal to them.'

At first Holwell could do nothing for fear of losing his hold on the iron bar of the window. A score of outstretched, supplicating hands were already vainly trying to supplant him and he knew that if he let go for an instant, he would be swept away from the only source of air. He gasped an appeal for help to Lushington and Cooke who were near him, and somehow managed to turn his head and face the middle of the room. Still keeping a grip on the iron bar, he cried out for silence.

One wonders how long it must have taken before he was able to bring momentary quiet into that confusion of struggling, dying men, how Holwell bore the physical agony, his body twisted as he peered into the room, one arm still gripping the bar. But it seems that at last he managed to quieten them and one can picture Holwell, his face illuminated by the glare of the fires through the tiny windows.   One can see, too, the moaning men trodden underfoot, the chaplain slowly dying at the far end of the room, Mary Carey huddled on a corner of the platform.   Lushington and Cooke were struggling to place themselves as a physical barrier between Holwell and the men near-by.   Clayton was already dead, his upturned face close to Lushington's feet, and Witherington was still fighting for a place at the other window. And yet this remarkable man of forty-five (old by Calcutta standards) still had the physical strength to fight for his own life, and the moral reserves and strength of character powerful enough to make him struggle to save his fellow men, strong enough to impel each man to listen.

'I begged and entreated, that as they had paid ready obedience to me in the day, they would now for their own sakes, and the sakes of those who were dear to them and were interested in the preservation of their lives, regard the advice I had to give them.'

Next morning, he promised them, will 'give us air and liberty'.   Looking at that sea of silenced, terrified faces reflected in the scarlet glow, he warned them that the only hope of survival lay in remaining absolutely calm. Each movement, each outburst of anger, must inevitably diminish their chances, but there was still a chance of life —a chance too of freedom—if they would promise him 'to curb as much as possible every agitation of mind and body, as raving and giving a loose to their passions could answer no purpose but that of hastening their destruction.'

Nothing can demonstrate Holwell's remarkable powers of leadership more clearly than the fact that this appeal had an immediate effect.   For a time there was com-

parative quiet, broken only by the cries and groans of the
wounded, and as Holwell turned to the window to gasp
in some of the hot night air, he had a few minutes to
reflect, to admit to himself what he had not dared tell
the others; that he could see no possibility of living
through the night. His duty had been to try and calm
the men, to offer them a fragment of hope, but as for
himself, 'death, attended with the most cruel train of
circumstances, I plainly perceived must prove our
inevitable destiny'.

Yet Holwell was far from giving up the struggle.
Among the guards near his window he had noticed a
man who seemed to 'carry some compassion for us in his
countenance'. From behind the bars Holwell beckoned
him to come closer. His sweat-streaked face peering
through the tiny window, the persuasive urgency with
which he spoke, must have influenced the guard no less
than the bribe—for Holwell offered the man a thousand
rupees, to be paid next morning, if he would go and find
a responsible officer and explain their terrible plight.
They did not ask for freedom that night; only that they
might be split into two groups and confined in separate
rooms.

A thousand rupees was a fortune, and Holwell was
certain the guard would trust an Englishman. After some
hesitation, the man agreed and, telling Holwell to wait
by the window, loped off along the arcade and disappeared into the darkness.

In a few minutes he returned, and whispered through
the window that nothing could be done. Behind him,
Holwell could hear the sounds of panic rising as the
prisoners began to mutter and shout again. It would be
difficult to control them much longer. Desperately he
asked the guard to try again. He even offered to double
the bribe—and again the guard ran off. There is no

doubt he genuinely tried to help the prisoners—but again he failed. 'He returned soon and (with I believe much pity and concern) told me it was not practicable.' Nothing could be done, the guard explained, without orders from the Nabob himself. And the Nabob was asleep. Nobody dared to wake him.

It was fateful news. Less than an hour had passed since the door of the Black Hole had been locked, but already every man among the survivors had broken out 'into a perspiration so profuse you can form no idea of it', which had the effect of bringing on a raging thirst, in addition to the desperate desire for air.

Someone cried out from among the sweat-drenched bodies which supported one another that there would be more room if everyone took off his clothes, and immediately those able to move started to strip. Most had already lost their heavy coats, but now that there was more space for those standing because of the many dead bodies on the floor, each man tore off his shirt and some even managed to pull off breeches so that, though Holwell and one or two others kept on their clothes, 'in a few minutes I believe every man was stripped.'

'For a little time they flattered themselves with having gained a mighty advantage,' but in fact the sweat streaming off the naked men packed so closely together acted as a sort of fatal lubricant. It was more difficult now for the weaker men to remain standing. Before, they had been able to clutch at their neighbour's clothes for support, but now when a fainting man reached out for something to clutch, his fingers merely slithered off slippery skin.

Not every man, however, collapsed on to the floor as he died, for in some corners the prisoners were so tightly packed they remained buoyed up in a grotesque standing position long after they had suffocated, slumping to the ground only hours later as others on the fringe slid downwards and the pressure eased with the addition of a few extra inches of space. For a time it was impossible to tell the dead from the living since the corpses were held upright, rigid as men on parade.

Many of the survivors had been thrown into the Hole still wearing their three-cornered hats, and it was not long before one of them had managed to wriggle an arm above his head, lift his hat and start fanning himself. Within a few seconds everyone was fighting desperately to follow his example. Arms were crushed, eyes were gouged, heads were cut open as men fought like animals to get their hats above their heads. Fighting, grunting, gasping and dying, only one thought seemed uppermost in their minds. Yet this apparently sensible move had most disastrous results for soon 'every hat was put in motion to produce a circulation of air' and the very effort of waving their hats in the cramped, restricted positions exhausted their energy and made the men sweat more than ever. Soon some whom the fanning had worn out were unable to get their arms down again, so that several died standing up in the most macabre positions, as though holding up their arms and hats in gestures of farewell.

Holwell is vague about the time it took for the first fifty or so men to die. How could he have known exactly? He was unable to see properly what was going on. One must remember that this dreadful battle against suffocation was fought in a temperature of nearly a hundred degrees, that the walls as well as the naked men were dripping with moisture and the only light depended on the flickering flames outside, as uncertain as the mantle of an old-fashioned gas-lamp popping in and out; there can be little doubt, however, that at least fifty must have succumbed within the first hour.

Now Lieutenant Baillie, who was directly behind Holwell, suddenly thought of a new idea, shouting out that each man would have more air if he squatted on his hams, and 'as they were truly in the situation of drowning wretches, no wonder they caught at everything that bore a flattering appearance of saving them.'

But once again the plan had disastrous results, for no man could sit on his haunches for long, and as Holwell could see in the dim light, 'many of the poor creatures, whose natural strength was less than others, could not immediately recover their legs [and] fell to rise no more; for they were instantly trod to death or suffocated.' Others who squatted found themselves so tightly wedged that they could not rise and they too were suffocated.

All this had happened in an hour or so—an hour that must have seemed endless. Holwell probably still hoped that pity for their plight would secure a merciful release. Those by the windows continued to shout, hoping for a miracle, but in vain. For the most part, however, the wretched prisoners—a third of their number already dead—must have existed in a state of semi-delirium in which they could not possibly realize what they were doing or how time was passing.

By nine o'clock 'every man's thirst had grown intolerable'. Respiration was becoming even more difficult, but Holwell determined not to give up hope and clung desperately to his place. 'By keeping my face between two of the bars', he recalled, 'I obtained air enough to give my lungs easy play, though my perspiration was excessive, and thirst commencing.' But already 'so strong an urinous volatile effluvia' were suffocating the small prison that he found he could no longer turn his head towards the interior of the Black Hole for more than a few seconds at a time.

Again and again the prisoners made desperate attempts to force the door—invariably without success. Next, some of them began hurling insults at the guards in the hope of provoking them to open fire and at least put an end to the nightmare. But the guards ignored them—until the men's piteous and insistent cries for 'Water! Water!' made the old guard whom Holwell had tried to bribe take pity on them.

Despite his own thirst, this was just what Holwell had dreaded. To his horror, he watched as the guard 'ordered the people to bring some skins of water, little dreaming, I believe of its fatal effects. I foresaw it would prove the ruin of the small chance left us.' Holwell's medical knowledge left him in little doubt that water itself could do nothing to assuage their raging thirst, but only accentuate the danger and lead to fighting.

With his face pressed to the bars, Holwell shouted to the guard to desist, but the old man apparently did not hear, and after a few minutes 'the water appeared. Words cannot paint to you the universal agitation and raving the sight of it threw us into. I had flattered myself that some, by preserving an equal temper of mind, might out-live the night; but now the reflection that gave me the greatest pain was that I saw no possibility of one escaping to tell the dismal tale.'

As every man fought to reach the window—and the water—Holwell tried to control the fighting that inevitably broke out. The only containers suitable for distributing the precious liquid were hats which Holwell and Lushington pushed through the bars so that the guards could fill them from the skins. These were almost useless. 'Though we brought full hats between the bars, there ensued such violent struggles and frequent contests to get at it that, before it reached the lips of anyone, there would scarcely be a small tea-cup full left in them.

These supplies, like sprinkling water on fire, only served to feed and raise the flame.'

Time after time whole hatfuls of water were spilled. Men fought like maniacs, dipped their hands into the empty felts, then licked them. The urge to drink was so desperate that several men at the other window left it—abandoning their only chance of air and life—and 'pressed down on those in their way . . . and trampled them to death' as they tried to reach Holwell's window.

'Oh! My dear Sir,' wrote Holwell, 'how shall I give you a conception of what I felt at the cries and ravings of those in the remoter parts of the prison, who could not entertain a probable hope of obtaining a drop, yet could not divert themselves of expectation, however unavailing! And others calling on me by the tender considerations of friendship and affection, and who knew they were really dear to me. Think, if possible, what my heart must have suffered at seeing their distress, without having it in my power to relieve them; for the confusion now became general and horrid.'

And now the situation grew rapidly worse, for it soon dawned on the other guards who had witnessed the old sentry's humane action without interest that by fetching more water—most of which they knew would be lost—they could watch a scene they had never believed possible: here were the all-powerful English, the soldiers thought to be invincible, the officers whose courage and dignity were a byword, fighting like wild animals. Such a spectacle had never been seen before, and more and more water was passed in while scores of guards came running to watch.

For two hours, with more men dying at their feet, the desperate prisoners fought for a few drops of water, while the guards jeered and encouraged them. 'They took care to keep us supplied with water', Holwell wrote, 'that they might have the satisfaction of seeing us fight for it, as they phrased it, and held up lights to the bars that they might lose no part of the inhuman diversion.'

Holwell himself, though firmly refusing water, fought to give it to the others by passing the hats of precious liquid into the Hole, but the pressure against him, the ruthless struggle of those nearest to him fighting for air, was beginning to tell. 'From about nine to near eleven, I sustained this cruel scene and painful situation, still supplying them with water, though my legs were almost broke with the weight against them. By this time I was very near pressed to death.'

And now the deaths began to come swiftly. Two wounded officers who had gained the window with Holwell in the first moments and who had helped to fill the hats were soon suffocated and crushed to death. Lieutenant Baillie was the next to die. Then it was Witherington's turn—foolish, indolent Witherington—who collapsed at Holwell's side and slipped down to vanish beneath the trampling feet 'of every corporal or common soldier who, by the help of more robust constitutions, had forced their way to the window'.

Holwell himself had almost reached the end of his strength. 'I became so pressed and wedged up I was deprived of all emotion.' The bodies of the dead were almost up to his knees—and almost every one of them had been his friend. At times, as he moved, he was conscious of unavoidably treading on them—not only on the bodies, but on their faces.

Perhaps this was the crucial moment, for it was now he decided he could hold out no longer and, turning to the survivors, 'I called to them and begged, as the last instance of their regard, they would remove the pressure upon me, and permit me to retire out of the window to die in quiet.'

Some of the men gave way, forming a minute passage into the centre of the room where there was a fraction more space, which suddenly increased as the guards, anxious to see more fighting, started bringing water to the second window. Immediately the strongest prisoners forced their way towards it, giving Holwell a chance to reach the platform. 'I travelled over the dead,' he wrote, as he somehow fought his way to the far end of the room. Here he found a small space near Gervas Bellamy who was lying next to John, both barely alive. Holwell bent over them, but though their eyes were open neither was able to speak. As he stood up, he noticed Dumbleton on the edge of the platform near Mary Carey. Even as he began to speak to the man, the notary collapsed and died.

At almost the same moment, Edward Eyre, a twenty-eight-year-old storekeeper, known for his wit, 'came staggering over the dead to me, and, with his usual coolness and good nature asked me how I did; but fell and expired before I had time to make him a reply.'

Holwell clambered on the platform, lay down on a pile of corpses and waited for the end. But now something quite unexpected occurred. He had been resigned to thirst and suffocation as an inevitable accompaniment to death, but within ten minutes of sinking down on his grisly couch of dead bodies, he was seized with excruciating pains in the chest. They hit him with the force of hammer blows and his reaction was immediate. As a doctor, he must have known the symptoms, for he recalled that he 'had the grief to see death not so near me as I hoped'. Worn down with strain and suffering, he had been fatalistically resigned to relapse into the unconsciousness which would precede death. But this agonizing pain galvanized him into an instinctive resolve not to die this way, and 'I instantly determined to push for the window opposite me; and by an effort of double the strength I ever before possessed' Holwell did manage to get back to a window, and after a few gulps of air his pains began to subside.

The fact that Holwell reached the window again is extraordinary, but one must bear in mind that Holwell's account has several omissions. Possibly an increasing number of men climbed on the platform; many of the dead may well have been pushed underneath it.

Pressed once again against the bars, Holwell now discovered for the first time he had a raging thirst, and kept his mouth moist by sucking the perspiration from his shirt-sleeves 'and catching the drops as they fell like heavy rain from my head and face'.

The faithful Lushington, close at hand, saw Holwell sucking his shirt. He would have liked to follow his example, but unfortunately he had thrown his away when everybody stripped, so all he could do was steal an occasional drop of sweat from Holwell's sleeve. It is the only time in his chronicle when Holwell adds a touch of humour. 'I was observed by one of my miserable companions on the right of me in the expedient of allaying my thirst by sucking my shirt-sleeves,' he wrote. 'He took the hint and robbed me from time to time of a considerable part of my store; though, after I detected him, I had ever the address to begin on that sleeve first when I thought my reservoirs were sufficiently replenished, and our mouths and noses often met in the contest. This plunderer . . . was a worthy young man in the service, Mr Lushington, one of the few who escaped from death, and has since paid me the compliment of assuring me he believed he owed his own life to the many comfortable draughts he had from my sleeves!'

As the hours wore on, the fighting and struggling must have died down to some extent. Many men were in a stupor, and no one could tell the dead from the living.

But certainly, as more and more fell to the ground, there must gradually have become more room for movement, for by now the floor was completely covered with prone and lifeless bodies.

Those 'who had yet some strength and vigour left made a last effort for the windows, and several succeeded by leaping and scrambling over the backs and heads of those in the first ranks, and got hold of the bars, from which tnere was no removing them. Many to the right and left sank with the violent pressure, and were soon suffocated; for now a steam arose from the living and the dead, which affected us in all its circumstances as if we were forcibly held with our heads over a bowl full of strong volatile spirit of hartshorn until suffocated.'

Many men had been trying to drink their own urine (including Holwell at one stage), and the stench mingling with the horrible odours from the trampled dead was so overpowering that Holwell dared not move his head from the window for more than a few seconds at a time, even though his hold on the bar was endangered by the weight of a heavy Dutch soldier who had clambered on top of him to get near the window and who had 'his knees in my back, and the pressure of his whole body on my head'.

For three hours the Dutchman perched on Holwell, keeping his balance by holding on to Holwell's head, while another tried to scramble on his right shoulder. Holwell tried everything to rid himself of the burden that was slowly weighing him down. He could feel himself sagging. The strain on his legs and knees must have been intolerable and his back felt as though it were being broken. By two o'clock in the morning he knew himself on the verge of collapse. Nothing could dislodge the man, and only by superhuman efforts was Holwell managing to keep upright.

Every instinct told him the end was near. When the agony had become unbearable—when he felt the last of his strength evaporating—with the weight now almost breaking his back, Holwell determined to take the quick way out. He remembered he had a penknife in his pocket. Were he able to reach the pocket of his trouser and get the knife out, he could open one of his arteries and 'finish a system no longer to be borne'. Cramped and pressed as he was, it must have taken a long time, but somehow Holwell in the end managed to extract the knife from his pocket. He was actually endeavouring to open it when he changed his mind.

It is easy for some of Holwell's critics to suggest that the magistrate appears to have spent a great deal of his time in the Black Hole vacillating whether to live or die, but when one recalls the frightfulness of that long, dark, flame-lit night, one wonders why Holwell should have been any less delirious or half-mad than the others. 'Heaven interposed,' was all he said later, 'and restored me to fresh spirits and resolution, with an abhorrence of the act of cowardice I was just going to commit.'

But Heaven must have seemed very far distant as Holwell summoned the last ounces of his rapidly flagging strength in a last desperate effort to rid himself of the Dutchman. It was useless. And what made it worse was the knowledge that sooner or later he must sink to the floor, and then what would happen? He seems to have been animated by a horror of others walking over his dead body, and the prospect of this hulk of a Dutch soldier standing perhaps on his face after he had died was unspeakable. Yet he had to move—he could not last much longer where he was.

Though time had ceased to have any meaning for the prisoners, we know that it was by now after one a.m. They had been cooped up for over five hours, and Holwell's mind must have been in torment, when he suddenly caught sight of Carey, who had left his wife (obviously able to bear the night more easily than the English) on the platform, and was now fighting for a place near the window. Holwell saw immediately that Carey, who 'had behaved with much bravery during the siege [and] had long been raving for water and air', was near the end. If he didn't get air soon he would die.

Holwell shouted to him, and, hearing and recognizing his voice, Carey began to fight to move over and join him. Carey was young and strong. Should he be capable of taking Holwell's place, the fresh air would revive him and he might well be able to survive despite the desperate throng around the window. Once he was there, Holwell had already decided to return to the platform.

Step by desperate step, Carey forced his way through to Holwell's side, but just as they were ready to change places, the Dutch soldier, with a grunt, slid down from Holwell's shoulders, shoved him aside and seized the bars. Neither Carey nor Holwell possessed the strength to force him away. And now there seemed no alternative but to force their way back towards Mary on the platform. With Carey in front, they began to fight their way into the centre of the room. It was the final effort of this stout-hearted sailor who had fought so gallantly throughout the siege. Half-dying, he summoned his last reserves of strength to force a passage for Holwell, who admits frankly that 'had he not retired with me, I should never have been able to have forced my way'.

Amid the macabre throng, many of the dead were still upright. Thrusting them aside, they had all but reached the platform when Carey noticed Leach, the carpenter. His face was hardly visible, but it was not until he had touched him that Carey realized the old man was dead —standing like so many others, as Holwell recalled, 'unable to fall by the throng and equal pressure round'.

Finally the two men reached the platform, and Carey managed to clamber up next to Mary. It was obvious to Holwell that nothing could be done for Carey now. As he watched helplessly, poor Carey laid himself down in Mary's arms. One minute he was alive and gasping. The next he was dead; at least 'his death', according to Holwell, 'was very sudden'.

All this had taken nearly an hour of desperate struggle, and it was now nearly two a.m. The frightful night had already taken a heavy toll, probably close on a hundred. One can imagine Holwell, eyes glazed, the moment poor Carey died. Almost every man he knew was now dead. It seemed an age since Clayton had died. Then there had been the terrifying sight of Leach, standing though a corpse on his two feet.

Is it any wonder Holwell despaired? Then, just below the platform, he saw the face of the man whom he was most anxious to find—his old friend Gervas. It was just possible to discern John's face beside him. Both seemed asleep, their backs to the wall, and for one wild, excited moment, Holwell perhaps experienced hope. He managed to scramble across the intervening bodies. Only one glance was necessary to assure him that both were dead. One wonders if Holwell remembered a moment less than a week ago when Gervas had said that if he had to die he hoped it would be with his favourite son. They were lying now, propped against the back wall, as though peacefully asleep. Gervas had a little smile on his face. John was wedged close beside him as though determined to stay near his father to the end. Each was holding the other's hand.

Holwell was unable to bear the sight. Here was the man who had been his closest friend in Calcutta, his hand clasped trustingly and infinitely pathetically in that of his son. It seemed the end. Choking with despair, Holwell clambered over the dead bodies back on to the platform, and climbed on it close to Mary and her dead husband.

He was ready to die, and this time unconsciousness was swift in coming. The last thing Holwell recollected before he lost consciousness was that as he lay down the broad sash round his waist that served as belt felt uncomfortable. He untied it, he remembered later, and threw it away.

Few details are available to give us any idea of the ensuing hours. Holwell, dead to all appearances, lay all but covered by a pile of corpses. What passed now during these last nightmare hours before dawn is based on hearsay. One is indeed inclined to believe with Holwell that the survivors' accounts were so excessively absurd and contradictory 'as to convince me very few of them retained their senses'.

As dawn approached, less than thirty men were still alive. Among the survivors was Lushington, whose youth (as much as Holwell's 'copious draughts') must have helped him to live. But it was the windows which had proved the source of survival. John Cooke—thirteen years older than Lushington—had managed to secure a place beside him there. Captain Mills still clung to a place at the neighbouring bars. Through them, the survivors could see that the flames outside were dying down. At dawn the gutted, blackened carcass, 'the finest piece of architecture in all Bengal', the Governor's House, was still smoking and lit by flame.

The few survivors, now dazed, exhausted, choking and gasping with the odour of putrefying corpses, begged the guards to open the door. In their despair they offered to be manacled, chained—any indignity to be free of that terrible room with its foetid stench of death.

Every plea was refused. Then Cooke suddenly thought of Holwell. None of the survivors had seen him for hours, but should he, by any unlikely chance, still be alive, his appearance at the window might lend authority to their entreaties. It is highly to the credit of Cooke and Lushington that even though the chances of finding Holwell alive seemed so remote they unhesitatingly left their precious positions by the window and stumbled back over the corpses, by now three or four deep over the entire floor.

It was a grotesque and horrible mission. In the half-light it was necessary to examine each corpse and peer closely at the contorted faces in their search for the magistrate. Panting, gasping, retching, they turned each body over, piling them behind as they moved farther into the prison. Then Lushington remembered that Holwell had been wearing a shirt. And this they kept in mind as they searched towards the back of the room, discovering the bodies of the Bellamys, near the platform, still clasping hands in death, and finding Mary Carey, long past weeping, cradling Peter's dead body in her arms. For the moment she was beyond speech. Could they do anything to help? She was unable to answer their questions.

Close to her, beneath a mound of bodies, Cooke caught a glimpse of a shirt: on the floor beneath the platform was the sash Holwell had discarded. Frantically they pulled away the bodies which lay across the magistrate. At last they uncovered his face. But Holwell appeared dead, although Cooke believed he detected some sign of life. The two men half dragged, half carried the magistrate over a carpet of bodies towards the window, shouting in their enfeebled voices to the others to make room so that they could show the magistrate to the guards.

Not a man at the window seemed disposed to give up his place. It may have crossed Lushington's mind to pull them down by force but by this time it was beyond his power. Instead, both he and Cooke begged and cajoled the men blocking the window to give way, for by now Holwell was showing distinct signs of life.

For a moment they laid him on a pile of corpses while they crawled to the other window. Here they were more fortunate. No arguments were necessary to convince Captain Mills that their only chance of survival depended on the magistrate's presence at the window to persuade the guards to release them before the stench and lack of air finished off the few survivors. Mills willingly offered to give up his place, and now Lushington and Cooke dragged Holwell to the window and propped him up against the bars, holding him in place with their own exhausted bodies. Though he was still unconscious, he was alive.

About this time it seems that the Nabob first heard of the catastrophe. We do not know how long Lushington and Cooke ranted at the guards from behind Holwell's still insensible body, but it seems that their pleas must have coincided with the rumours reaching the Nabob, for at once he sent an officer to enquire if Holwell were still alive. Without doubt he was still determined to find the treasure and was convinced Holwell knew where it was hidden.

With what eagerness Lushington and Cooke must have thrust Holwell up against the bars as the officer arrived! One can imagine their pale, exhausted faces, the urgent sentences which informed him the magistrate was barely living but might be saved if the door were opened immediately.

The smell issuing from the Black Hole as well as the sight of their desperate faces must have deeply affected the officer, for he ran all the way to Wedderburn's house where the Nabob had set up his headquarters for the night and must have given a graphic account of Holwell's condition, for Siraj-Uddaula jumped off his couch, strode across the room and gave orders for the Black Hole to be opened instantly.

Long before the officer returned, however, the fresh morning air gasped through the prison bars had begun to revive Holwell and 'soon brought me to life; and [in] a few minutes I was restored to my sight and senses'.

But even when the officer was there and the door was to be opened, one final and macabre obstacle faced the survivors. For the door opened inwards, and all the efforts of the guards proved unavailing against the barricade of dead bodies. It was left to the few weakened prisoners who somehow found enough strength to drag away the dead who blocked their path to freedom. So far gone were they now that it took them twenty terrible minutes.

At last it was done. At six a.m., ten hours after the lock had been turned in the door, twenty-two men and one woman staggered across the bodies of their companions and stumbled out, one at a time, into the fresh air of the parade-ground, leaving a hundred and twenty-three dead behind.

CHAPTER TEN

Retribution

Monday, June 21, and later

Among the Nabob's many failings was a trait which oddly enough he had in common with the British who had composed the unfortunate garrison: a tendency to underrate the enemy. This fatal trait had already cost his enemies Calcutta; soon it was to lose the Nabob the whole of Bengal.

Having virtually exterminated the defenders of the Fort who had not already fled, and thoroughly terrorized the inhabitants of Calcutta, who were now beginning to creep back into the devastated city, the Nabob seems to have imagined that the question of the British in Calcutta had been most satisfactorily settled once and for all. At no time does the thought appear to have entered his head that his action was likely to have the most violent repercussions, nor that the British, outraged and bent on vengeance, were to prove a very different foe from the indolent, incompetent figures he had known until now.

It is hardly surprising. The Nabob was totally uninformed about that almost mythical island thousands of miles away, and not unnaturally concluded that the size of the small European settlements in his domain conveniently reflected equally small and vulnerable countries.

Since he could not possibly visualize the might of Britain, let alone the size, strength and resources of Europe, it is perhaps not surprising that he underestimated them.

The deserters, led by Drake, had sailed down-river for twenty-seven miles to a place called Fulta, and a refugee camp had been established there. Yet the Nabob had made only one serious attempt to prevent the deserters' vessels reaching Fulta. Apart from this, and a skirmish or two, he apparently made no efforts to consolidate his position once and for all by driving the British right out of Bengal. He had sworn to take Calcutta, he had done so—and that was that. It naturally never occurred to him that he might very shortly lose it, nor even that the refugee camp at Fulta, less than thirty miles from Calcutta, could be a spring-board for a counter-attack.

This fatal but understandable state of mind was best summed up by Jean Law, the chief of the French settlement at nearby Chandernagore, who wrote that 'Siraj-Uddaula had the most extravagant contempt for Europeans; a pair of slippers, said he, is all that is needed to govern them. Their number, according to him, could not in all Europe come up to more than ten or twelve thousand men. What fear, then, could he have of the British nation, which assuredly could not present to his mind more than a quarter of the whole? He was, therefore, very far from thinking that the British could entertain the idea of re-establishing themselves by force. To humiliate themselves—to offer money with one hand, and receive joyfully with the other his permission to re-establish themselves—was the whole project which he could naturally suppose them to have formed. It is to this idea, without doubt, that the tranquillity in which he left them at Fulta is due.'

From the moment the survivors tottered and stumbled

out of the Black Hole to throw themselves gasping on the parade-ground, the Nabob's attitude appears to have been unambitious: the siege was over, the fighting had ended, now was the moment for the victors to divide the spoils of war. He ordered a mosque to be built near the east gate and promptly re-named the city Alinagar, a name destined to last only a few months before it once again became Calcutta.

Smoke was still rising from the blackened, gutted ruins of Fort William on this first day of peace, and it was hard to believe that little more than a week ago its inhabitants had been engaged in peaceful pursuits, sharing their work with steadfast and true men they believed would be their companions for years to come.

Almost all the steadfast and true were gone, killed in the fighting or suffocated in the nightmare of the Black Hole, and one can imagine the thoughts of Henry Lushington as he watched the few survivors slowly returning to life. It must have seemed a whole decade of experience since Janniko had been killed; since Thoresby had been shot at Perrin's; since the desperate attempt to hold Minchin's house, when Smith and Wilkinson had been cut to pieces; since the suicide of the elder Bellamy boy; even since the last battle, with Blagg and Piccard in their scarlet coats dying in a blaze of glory.

Lying on the parade-ground, he observed that Indian troops were already dragging out the dead from the Black Hole and loading them on to rough carts. Though he was unable to identify all the corpses, there was a horrible and urgent fascination in anxiously scanning each new body. He recognized Carey, caught a glimpse of old Bellamy, and saw Clayton's body tossed unceremoniously on to a cart where it lay on top of Witherington's. The carts moved off. Later he was to learn that all the bodies had been taken to the ditch which the

garrison had cut through The Park, dumped into it and
covered with earth.

The great majority of the survivors were now too ill
to move and were left unguarded so that Lushington,
younger and stronger than the others, was able to
stagger across the shambles of the parade-ground to
Writers' Row where he had lived for nearly three years.

He found it razed to the ground. Here and there a
fragment of wall remained, here and there he would find
a piece of furniture when he poked the ashes. As he
peered into the skeleton of one room he saw the twisted
iron cot on which Sarah Mapletoft had given birth to
her daughter. Close by, the armoury and laboratory had
been burned out too, and the treasure-room looked as
though a horde of marauders had wrecked it in a frenzy
of frustrated rage. As he stumbled back into the sunlight of the parade-ground he saw that the Nabob's troops
were still searching for loot and plunder, stripping corpses
of anything of value from a button to a single shoe. When
he returned to his companions he saw an Indian carrying
yet another body out of the Black Hole, humping it over
his shoulder with the same unconcern a butcher might
display with a carcass. Lushington recognized a familiar
splash of colour. Going nearer, he saw the corpse was
that of a soldier wearing the sash Holwell had thrown
away.

But war never ends tidily, and though most of the
survivors were now left in peace to nurse their grief and
gasp their way back to tolerable health, their individual
problems had hardly begun. Perhaps it was too early to
realize the enormity of the task of building new lives
out of the wreckage they had inherited. Many would
return to England, but not one of the survivors on the
parade-ground at that moment could have believed that
those who were to stay on would live to see the cowards

and deserters—whom they so despised—astonishingly forgiven and reinstated in the Company.

But all that still lay in the future. First there was retribution.

Before many hours had gone by, the Nabob sent for Holwell, who, still half-conscious, was too weak to stand. It must have been a macabre scene. Siraj-Uddaula beckoned for a retainer to bring a pile of large books on which Holwell was placed while the Nabob, leaning forward eagerly, continued to probe him as to where the treasure was hidden.

For more than an hour the Nabob persisted in his interrogation and his choler mounted to fever pitch as he dashed aside the exhausted Holwell's denial of its existence. In the face of these continued denials, he decreed that Holwell must remain a prisoner until the treasure was disgorged. An officer then stepped forward with an even sterner threat—Holwell was to be blown from the mouth of a cannon were the immediate where-abouts of the treasure not disclosed.

But what could Holwell say? He had no idea where the treasure was situated—if indeed there was any treasure at all. For all he knew, it might possibly have been stolen by some of the deserters. It would not have been difficult to load the chests of coral and plate on privately owned boats at the very start of the siege.

All these theories were of no interest to a Nabob not only thwarted but growing increasingly angry. After another hour of questioning and threats he ordered Hol-well to be clapped in irons. For some reason which has never been explained, he picked out three other survivors —apparently at random—and ordered them to be imprisoned with the magistrate.

As Holwell, still sitting on the pile of books, tried to remonstrate, the Nabob ordered Roy Doolub to parade the rest of the survivors. All but the unlucky four were given their freedom—on condition that they left Calcutta within the hour.

It must have been one of the most poignant moments of this dreadful story. As Holwell and his three companions were forced to stand, manacled like common prisoners, Lushington, Cooke, Mills and the other survivors were given a moment to say farewell to the man who had fought for them all and saved them all. Holwell's reaction must have been one of utter dismay. There was nothing the loyal Lushington and the others could do. They were quickly bundled away towards Surman's Gardens, and Holwell doubtless thought that he would not live to see any of them again. (All but two of those who were given their freedom eventually reached the refugees at Fulta.)

Holwell and his three fellow prisoners, protesting in vain, were thrown into a bullock cart and taken to Omichand's garden. The next day they were marched in irons beneath a blistering sun to the river bank, where after a night in the open they were loaded into a boat destined to go up-river towards the Nabob's capital of Murshidabad. This journey took the best part of two weeks in appalling conditions. Both Holwell and his companions were now covered in boils and were given virtually no food (which, as Holwell points out, probably saved their lives). They were not to reach Murshidabad until July 7, where they were thrown into a common prison where a week was to pass before the Nabob deigned to see them. Then, as Holwell recalled, 'the wretched spectacle we made must, I think, have made an impression in a breast the most brutal, and if he is capable of pity or contrition, his heart felt it then.'

Suddenly and almost unaccountably, the Nabob decided to release them, presumably because by now it must have dawned on him that Holwell knew nothing about the treasure. Despite bitter recriminations by Roy Doolub and St Jacques, who wanted Holwell returned as a hostage to Calcutta where, they insisted, 'the Governor would know how to make him give up the secret of the hidden treasure', their irons were cast off and they were set free. It is a curious insight into the character of the bloodthirsty Nabob that in a sudden burst of generosity he turned to his officers and said, 'It may be. If he has anything left, let him keep it. His sufferings have been great. He shall have his liberty.'

Hardly able to believe their good fortune, the four prisoners now contrived to make their own way to the near-by Dutch settlement, where they were fed and well-treated. Then the four men took a boat down-river until they were able to join the refugees at Fulta.

They reached Fulta in the second week of August. Their arrival in Fulta which was thronged not only with refugees, women and children, but with the deserters who had escaped, leaving Calcutta to its fate, must have astonished Holwell and his companions.

The place was little more than a settlement in a bend of the Hoogly, and though one or two vessels had been lost in sporadic fighting, the rest—numbering over a dozen—had congregated off the river bank. Five hundred refugees, including most of the leaders of Calcutta, were living in this squalid camp. One would have thought the deserters might have been shamed into silence, but in fact an extraordinary attempt had been made to re-create the authority and life of Calcutta before the siege.

Here Drake had now arrogantly assumed the dubious title of Governor. But the whole situation was a farce, for only a brief message had been sent to Madras recounting the fall of Calcutta. No official despatch detailing the events which had led to the catastrophe and its terrible sequel had yet reached the authorities for the simple reason that the Council members who had deserted were striving desperately to prevent the real truth seeping out.

Once again this inane and forlorn little group was inflated with its importance, still enmeshed in protocol and oblivious of the fact that the leading figures in it were now branded as cowards and deserters. They continued to waste their time arguing in a paralysis of inertia, while the women and children around them existed amid the most appallingly miserable conditions.

The monsoon had broken and now 'the want of convenient shelter, as well as the dread of being surprised', wrote the historian Orme, 'obliged them all to sleep on board the vessels, which were so crowded that all lay promiscuously on the decks, without shelter from the rains of the season, and for some time without a change of raiment, for none had brought any store away, and these hardships, inconsiderable as they may seem, were grievous to persons of whom the greatest part had lived many years in the gentle ease of India. Sickness likewise increased their sufferings, for the lower part of Bengal between the two arms of the Ganges [Ganges and Hoogly] is the most unhealthy country in the world, and many died of a malignant fever which infected all the vessels. But instead of alleviating their distresses by that spirit of mutual good will which is supposed to prevail amongst companions in misery, everyone turned his mind to invidious discussions of the causes which had produced their misfortune. All seemed to expect a day when they should be restored to Calcutta. The younger men in the Company's service, who had not held any post in the Government, endeavoured to fix every kind of blame on their superiors, whom they wished to see removed from their stations, to which they expected to succeed. At the same time, the Members of Council accused one another, and these examples gave rise to the same spirit of invective amongst those who could derive no benefit from such declamations.'

In this tragically farcical atmosphere of squabbling and intrigue, 'Mr Drake with an almost impudent lack of humour' had himself moved from the *Dodaldy* to the *Fort William*, which lay farther out in the river. Incredibly, he still insisted on all the trappings of office, even to a ceremonial salute of guns whenever he was rowed over to dine on another ship.

Very little information is available which throws light on the condition of the women and children—except that it appears they stood 'the fluxes and fevers' better than the men, who, according to the records of life at Fulta, were occupied almost to a point of obsession in manu-facturing excuses to defend their 'honour'.

Manningham, Frankland and Minchin among them were successful in their dubious efforts if only because Manningham himself was entrusted to carry the vital explanatory letter to Madras—a document designed to exculpate the cowardly actions of Governor and deserter alike, since Manningham in person would be available to pour soothing explanations into credulous ears in Madras.

In the circumstances it is hardly surprising he should have been chosen by the other leaders, yet when the announcement was first made, it caused such an uproar that Drake, on board the *Fort William*, was presented with a letter of protest, signed by the junior officers and all the civilians. This document read:

'Honourable Sir: Understanding that Charles Man-ningham, Esq. intends going to Madras in order to represent the unfortunate loss of Calcutta and the situation of the remaining part of the Colony; as that gentleman and Mr Frankland left the place before any retreat was agreed to and afterwards refused joining your Councils when sent for, contrary to both their duty and honour, we are of the opinion that either of those gentlemen are most unfit to represent transactions, which (as they absented themselves) they must know very little of, and therefore request that neither they nor any member of Council may be permitted to abandon the remains of the Colony and the Company's effects scattered throughout the country.'

Cornered, and caught at a disadvantage, Drake's reaction was typical. He blandly reassured the refugees he had changed his mind and would send neither Manningham nor Frankland—and half an hour later he broke his word.

Was Drake entirely to blame? It seems that Manningham bluntly blackmailed the signatories to the letter and warned them that since he would go whatever happened and would be the first man to reach Madras, their reputations would lie in his hands. How closely Drake and Manningham worked together in playing on the fears and emotions of the wretched survivors of the Council will never be known. All we know is that it was Manningham who went to Madras. As a sop to the opinions now violently voiced against the mission, Drake arranged for Lebeaume, who had recovered from his wounds, to accompany him.

Determined to maintain the dignity and authority of his official title, despite the tide of derision and ill-feeling now running against him, an unexpected aspect of Drake's character now became apparent. Doubtless conscious of the hostility so patently obvious in the crowded camp, the enormity of his actions in Calcutta seems to have borne most heavily upon him. Despite the knowledge that sooner or later censure and discredit awaited him, he none the less continued to exert what little authority was left to him and even had an odd and somewhat intriguing document nailed to the mast of every vessel lying in the river. It read:

'Advertisement to the late inhabitants of Calcutta and others under the protection of the English flag at Fulta and on board ships anchored off shore.

'Whereas it has been my request to the Gentlemen of Council that they will be pleased jointly or separately to acquaint me publickly of the censure that in their judgment I merit by the late misfortune that has befell our Settlement of Calcutta, and which they have assented to deliver in within one month from the date hereof, so I hope to be granted by you, gentlemen, the indulgence of being accused of such actions you may think me blameable in committing within that time, and that you will be pleased to deliver such your accusations founded on truth either to the Gentlemen in Council in their publick capacity, or addressed to any one separate member, or to him who is, gentlemen, your most obedient humble servant,   ROGER DRAKE, JNR.'

One or two survivors from the world where Drake had lorded it in Calcutta took advantage of his kind offer. The majority, however, reserved their fire for the court of enquiry which they knew inevitably must follow the disastrous bungling at Calcutta.

It is not the purpose of this book to recount the detailed story of the recapture of the city of Calcutta, nor the battle of Plassey that was to be fought a little later and was to change the fate of India in a day. The story of the Black Hole is now over, and we are concerned only with the fates of the men and women we have come to know so well.

First the Nabob himself. Here retribution was unexpectedly swift. As soon as the news of the fall of Calcutta reached Madras, an expedition was hastily organized to recapture the city and, moving with speed and despatch, actually achieved this aim during the month of January 1757. Calcutta—or what was left of it—was once again in British hands. A new fort was built on a site south of the old one, while Siraj-Uddaula was forced to sign a new treaty which ensured the settlement's safety and freedom to trade.

The Nabob not unnaturally retained an almost hysterical hatred for the British. When news of the outbreak of the Seven Years' War reached Bengal and he knew France and Britain were officially at war, it was very natural he should side with the French in India. His judgment, however, proved unwise, for the war gave Clive, who was commanding the British forces, an opportunity to capture the French settlement of Chandernagore, only twenty-one miles from Calcutta: perhaps even more important, the Nabob's open partisanship now provided an excellent excuse for intriguing to ensure his downfall.

Clive knew that many of the Nabob's officials were bitterly discontented, and it did not take him long to choose one of them, Mir Jaffir, and conspire secretly to offer him the throne of Bengal when the opportunity arrived. It arrived at Plassey.

On June 23, 1757, the famous battle was fought in which eight hundred Europeans and two thousand two hundred Indians under Clive routed the Nabob's unwieldy army of some fifty thousand men. In part this was due to the fact that the Indian troops under the command of Mir Jaffir (and for that matter Roy Doolub) merely looked on. British losses were sixty-five. The Nabob fled.

The political results of this vital skirmish were to endure for two centuries. Mir Jaffir became Nabob, Clive received a modest 'gift' of £234,000, and the British became the virtual rulers of Bengal.

Mounted on a fast dromedary, Siraj-Uddaula with a handful of loyal officers managed to reach his palace at Murshidabad, where he decided 'despite the pleas of his harem' to flee.

Already Mir Jaffir was searching for him. Hastily packing that useful and negotiable form of currency, 'a large casket of jewels', Siraj-Uddaula escaped by a rope dangling from an upper room of the palace. His favourite wife followed. Both were disguised in peasants' rags and were rowed up-river, eventually (and with a certain ironic justice) being forced to seek refuge in the hut of a dervish whose ears the Nabob had ordered to be cut off only a year previously.

It was nearly the end. The dervish betrayed him, and Siraj-Uddaula, 'Lord of the Lamp', was dragged back in chains to his own palace and at midnight was taken before Mir Jaffir. 'He crawled in the dust at Mir Jaffir's feet, begging for mercy.'

Only two more days were left to him. Some say that Siraj-Uddaula asked for a bath and was assassinated while bathing; others that Mir Jaffir's son (whom Clive described as 'a worthless young dog') ordered a servant to murder him while the other servants looked on, jeering.

The blood-spattered body of the man whose cruelty, avarice, bitterness and pettiness had cost him his country and provided the British with a pretext for building an Empire in India, was paraded through the streets the next day on a state elephant; the head was missing but accompanied the elephant on the point of a pike.

The fortunes of the sycophants and henchmen who had surrounded him during the days of brutality and cruelty leading up to the final holocaust in the Black Hole seem to have declined with their master's death.

Omichand had not long to live. As slimy as ever, this man who had helped betray the Fort endeavoured to creep back into British favour, and after the death of Siraj-Uddaula he seems to have been successful with Clive by stressing that he was pleased his masters had returned to Calcutta. Within two years he was dead; some accounts say of a fever in 1758, others claim he became a raving lunatic. It is hard to know which version is correct.

We have little information about the Nabob's chief lieutenants. St Jacques was left in charge of the Indian garrison at Calcutta but then disappears from all contemporary accounts, while Roy Doolub, though we know he was present at the battle of Plassey and 'stood neuter' (for he, like many others, had made his own terms with Clive), seems to fade away so that we lose all written trace. Nor do we know anything about the ultimate fate of Hedleburgh, except that after the betrayal of Fort William, this Dutch renegade officially entered the service of the Nabob.

Among the British, Captain Minchin was the only man actually to be dismissed following the official enquiry. The Court of Directors 'summoned him home immediately', but even at this moment Captain Minchin found it impossible to bow to authority and elected to remain in Bengal. He died in Calcutta on January 5, 1758.

Drake was to fare better. For some little time the Directors seem to have left his fate in abeyance, but by January 27, 1758—only three weeks after Minchin's death—the East India Company had resolved 'that Roger Drake, Esq., late President of Bengal, be continued in the Company's service, and remain as and at the head of the Senior Merchants and with their appointments, without interfering in the Company's affairs'.

It was a come-down, of course, for a senior merchant was one grade below a council member, but at least Drake was the chief senior merchant and 'this seems to be all that was done by the Court in the way of punishment for the loss of the finest Settlement they possessed in the Indies'.

If this indifference towards rank incompetence and cowardice seems strange, one must remember that the East India Company was above all things a trading concern, and the Directors in Leadenhall Street doubtless felt it a waste of time and money to drag witnesses back to England for a full-scale enquiry. Much of the evidence which emerged was contradictory in any case, and tinged with personal spite. The Directors were doubtless only too well aware in addition that a really searching enquiry might have laid the blame fairly and squarely on themselves and the policy of the Company. The only thing which really concerned them now was the resumption of trade. The whole affair had been painful, but 'in short, it was one of those unfortunate incidents which good business men would think best forgotten'.

Drake eventually retired, and presumably his wife died, for he married again—a Miss Henrietta Baker, the daughter of a clergyman. He died at Windsor on August 4, 1765.

Of the others we have only fragmentary information.

Drake was not the only lucky one. Manningham and Frankland were also reinstated and indeed in 1758 both were promoted. We have no record of Franklin after that date, but Manningham returned to England in 1772 to give evidence to the Government Committee set up 'to Enquire into the State of the East India Company.'

William Tooke, the youngster of twenty-five on whose caustic reports we have relied so much, had only a few more months to live. He fought bravely at the battle of Chandernagore a few months later and, according to Clive's journal, 'received a shot through his body, of which he soon died'.

Lebeaume, who had seen so much action when holding the gaol with Ensign Carstairs, was soon in action again after travelling with Manningham to Madras. Yet this Frenchman who was such an individualist was now to be troubled by divided loyalties, and by the time war had been officially declared between Britain and France, he must have been an unhappy man. He took part in the recapture of Calcutta, but in April 1757 was court-martialled by Clive and dismissed. He was restored to his former rank two months later, however, so it is safe to assume that his brief period of disgrace was due to conflicting loyalties during the attack on the French. It was doubtless for this reason that he resigned twelve months later, and we know no more about him after that.

Two faithful friends, both young, were to live only a few more years and then die together. They were Lushington, who had stood so staunchly by Holwell, and Ensign Carstairs, who had been wounded with Lebeaume at the gaol on that first awful day. Both were killed during the native uprising of 1763. Lushington was by then twenty-five; Carstairs was about thirty.

Cooke, the Company Secretary, who lived through the Black Hole and helped Lushington to drag Holwell to the window, was luckier. He was to have a long and distinguished career with the East India Company, rising to become a member of the Council.

Captain Mills, who gave up his place at the window in the Black Hole so that Holwell could be propped up and shown to the Nabob's officer, became Commodore of the Company's yacht at Calcutta, but achieved fame for a quite different reason. After his return to England (presumably on leave), 'he married a lady who loved him for the dangers he had passed'. This lady was Mrs Vincent, a celebrity on the English stage, who played Polly Peachum in *The Beggar's Opera* and was 'much admired for her melodious voice and amiable, simple disposition'.

In typical sailor fashion, Captain Mills wooed and won her, and then whisked her away from all the frivolities of the London stage to Bengal. They did eventually return to London, where, after the death of Mrs Mills, the captain lived alone to the age of eighty-nine, existing on a small pension from the Company after having frittered away his fortune on his beautiful wife, and dying in Camden Town in 1811.

Poor Dorothy Bellamy. It must have been a broken heart that killed her. She caught a fever and died at Fulta, not being strong enough to bear the shock of three deaths—her husband and two sons. We do not know what happened to her daughter Anna. Anne Mackett stayed with her husband, who was exonerated as a result of the enquiry and rose high in the ranks of the Company. Grant too was exonerated.

Among the men who died of fever at Fulta was the Reverend Mapletoft, so it is understandable that Mrs Mapletoft and her three young children—including Constantia, born during the siege—should leave for England as soon as a passage could be provided. There was nothing to keep Mapletoft's widow in a country she so obviously detested.

Another woman was to die within a year of the Black

Hole—the indomitable Lady Russell. There is some confusion about the time and place. She certainly reached Fulta after Leach had helped her to escape from Fort William, and we know she became very ill there. No reports, however, indicate that she actually died at Fulta. We only know that she died 'a few months after the Black Hole'.

In contrast, Mary Carey was to live until she was sixty. There are few details, though it does not seem that she was (as some have suggested) taken to the Nabob's harem, which is not surprising considering the Moslem respect for women. She remained in or near Calcutta, and after some years married again, an English officer named Weston by whom she had two sons and a daughter. Much later, after Weston had died, she reverted to the name of Carey. She died on March 28, 1801, and was buried in what was then the churchyard of the Catholic Cathedral in Calcutta.

Over a hundred years later—in 1907 when the Cathedral had been demolished and rebuilt elsewhere—the Governor of Bengal had a memorial tablet to mark the site of her grave placed on the wall of the Catholic Male Orphanage Schoolroom which now stood on the old site of the Cathedral. The inscription, in part, read: 'Near this tablet were interred the remains of Mrs Mary Carey, wife of Peter Carey, mariner . . . she had on the night of June 20, 1756, been confined in the Black Hole prison. She survived the tragedy, and of its survivors, was the last to die in India.'

We have one more memento of Mary. Hill, in his *Bengal 1756-57*, describes 'a well-executed miniature painted on the inside of the lid of a trinket box; it certainly testifies to the truth of what Holwell records about her appearance, for the artist has shown her in the full beauty of youth.'

Finally there is Holwell. This man whose example stands unique in a shabby tale of ineffectual command, who refused to surrender, rallied the survivors and fought to the end, was in such poor health on his release that he was sent home to England on sick leave as soon as possible, and it was on the voyage home, in the sloop *Syren*, that Holwell wrote his celebrated Black Hole letter.

He was not to remain long in England. Fully recovered, he was back by 1758—and this time the former surgeon, the former Zemindar, returned to India as Governor of Bengal. It was during his tour of office there that Holwell arranged for an obelisk to be constructed to the memory of his fellow sufferers in the Black Hole. This was erected in The Park, opposite the east gate of the Fort, close to the spot where their bodies were buried.

Holwell stayed only two years, and his decision to return to England in 1760 was no doubt due to the fact that he and Clive did not get on well together. Holwell settled first at Walton-on-Thames but later moved to Pinner in Middlesex, where he died in 1798, aged 87.

The obelisk which he left behind him had been constructed of brick and it was not long before it began to crumble. Further damaged by lightning, it was finally pulled down in 1821. It was later replaced by a marble replica.

With the coming of the Republic of India, this in turn has vanished. How many people today, crossing the busy streets and crowded squares of the Commonwealth's second largest city, realize how often they are treading the same ground that Holwell and his exhausted garrison fought so hard to defend two centuries ago; how often, each time they post a letter, they are standing on, or close to, the very spot where Gervas and John Bellamy died in the Black Hole?

Hardly a visiting Englishman can pause to think on such things these days. Yet though it is so far distant in time, hardly an Englishman has not learned the story of the Black Hole in his history books, and even for those few who remember it is hard to realize that, though a new India has been built on the old, though a new Calcutta has risen where Job Charnock first started to trade from a thatched hut, the ground beneath the new buildings is still the same, with the same Hoogly river flowing sluggishly past. The site of the siege lies today in the very heart of this great city of nearly seven million souls.

If you walk northwards along the famous Chowringhee Road, with the green of the great Maidan on your left and the Grand Hotel on your right, and then bear slightly left, you will come to Mission Row. The short street is not very wide but it is among the oldest in Calcutta. It is lined with houses and offices and there is no reason why you should give it a second glance; nor why, as you walk its quarter of a mile, you should realize that this street was once called Rope Walk.

Here, where now you can saunter past narrow buildings, dodging the hurrying citizens, their shirt-tails flapping outside their trousers, is the spot where Lady Russell once lived in the lonely splendour of her big house surrounded by its compound. A few steps farther on, a shop marks the site of Dumbleton the notary's house, from whose roof and windows the Nabob's troops began firing with such ferocity on to the east battery during the siege.

Mission Row leads straight into the north-east corner

of Dalhousie Square, and here at the junction stands St Andrew's Church. As you walk gratefully into the cool shade of its nave, it is strange to reflect that it is near this spot that Captain Clayton so ingloriously decided to retreat and abandon his eighteen-pounders after the magnificent stand by Lebeaume and Carstairs—for here, inside the church, is the site of the east battery.

The north side of Dalhousie Square leads you directly to the General Post Office, which has been built on part of the site of old Fort William. The Post Office is a massive edifice, with a dome of reinforced concrete well over two hundred feet high, an ironic memorial to the splendour of Drake's mansion which the prisoners could see burning during the night of the Black Hole.

At first there is nothing to remind one of the fierce battle that raged all around this area before Fort William fell; nothing to summon up a picture of the last hours, the final moments—Hedleburgh rushing through the Governor's House where today parcels are posted; Blagg and Piccard cut to pieces where now the inhabitants of modern Calcutta send their telegrams.

Post offices tend to be as neutral as abattoirs and this one is no exception. Its cavernous interior is full of echoes; the vast building is alive with frustrated citizens in a perpetual hurry, beneath the gaze of the staff who (in common with so many other post office staffs) look unutterably bored, due no doubt to the dilatory performance of their duties. Until recently, when structural alterations were made near the north-east corner of the Post Office, a black marble tablet marked the actual site of the Black Hole. Not far away, in the Post Office yard, there used to be fragments of the original arcades that lined the east wall, but they were demolished some years ago.

The Post Office is near the river, and even today you

can stand on the bank at the very place where Grant and Drake quarrelled as the adjutant tried to prevent the Governor from deserting. It was here too that Manningham vindictively prevented Mary Carey from going aboard the *Dodaldy*; a little farther up-river is the spot where the wretched Indians fleeing from the Fort were drowned or burned alive, victims of their own panic and the fire of the Nabob's troops. And farther north you can plainly see the famous Howrah Bridge that today spans the river. Somewhere between this bridge and where you stand, the *Prince George* crunched on to a sandbank and the last hope of evacuating the garrison vanished.

Otherwise there is little else to remind you of this moment of history about which most of us know so little and which many would prefer should be forgotten. If you walk away from the river, up Hastings Street, you quickly reach Council House Street; it was at the crossroads here that the south battery was erected, only to be evacuated before it had seen any action.

A short distance farther on stands the Great Eastern Hotel, its lobby packed with tourists fingering saris in the arcade shops, rushing to buy their souvenirs before aeroplanes whisk them off to another place, another country, where doubtless history was also written in blood, little realizing that this imposing hotel may well have been built on the site of Minchin's house, where Blagg and his colleagues held out for hours in the most heroic stand of the siege.

It must have been very close by, perhaps somewhere in the area now covered by neighbouring streets, that— while Smith and Wilkinson were cut to pieces in the last desperate minutes—Blagg led his men across the compound to the corner of The Park where Lushington was waiting with a six-pounder. And if you walk in that direction from the Great Eastern Hotel, you will come to the corner of Dalhousie Square in a matter of moments.

And in the centre of this Square—which was once The Park where Holwell and Bellamy used to meet and where the palanquins brought the English merchants and officials and their families for their evening walk—there is one souvenir of the past which has remained unchanged. It is the Great Tank, just as it was two centuries ago; a square, ornamental pond surrounded with flower gardens, and as you walk past it, the traffic rumbling up Council House Street on your left just as traffic of a very different kind once rumbled from the Armoury to the Fort, you will notice a pair of ancient Indian gardeners tending the shrubs and flowers in the square. When they want to water them, they crouch down carefully or wade into the water and dip their vessels into the Great Tank, just as their ancestors used to wade into the very same Tank searching for the carp and mullet stocked there to grace the table of Governor Drake.

The north side of Dalhousie Square follows the path of the old Avenue, along which Holwell and Grant galloped furiously to reach the east battery, only to rein in their horses in dismay at the sight of Clayton's disastrous retreat.

The Avenue down which the Nabob marched his troops has now been named Bowbazar Street, but it remains as long and straight as a ruler until it reaches the point where the Nabob assembled his troops near the Bread and Cheese Bungalow. Now you must take a taxi—for it is a long way—and then turn left along the Circular Road at Sealdah railway station, until eventually you arrive at a quiet oasis in this ant-like metropolis. It is a spot to which guides like to take tourists, for perhaps even they can hardly believe such a peaceful spot exists amid all the bustle and activity of modern Calcutta.

It is near Cornwallis Square that a turning into a quieter street, almost a lane, brings you to a gate leading into a garden containing the Jain temples of Omichand's religion. This garden today is called Badri Das, and it is here that the Nabob set up his first camp following his march from Cossimbazar. It was here that he ordered all the vulgar furniture thrown out of Omichand's house It was in that house, now long vanished, that Roy Doolub woke him in the dead of night with the news that the dying Jaggernath had arrived bearing the vital information that the Maratha Ditch had not been completed to encircle the city; it was here too that Holwell was brought in a bullock cart the morning after his release from the Black Hole. This was Omichand's garden.

It is not altogether fashionable now for the guide to dwell on the events that took place in this remote corner of Calcutta. He will almost certainly refrain from mentioning (even if he knows) that this was once the headquarters of a cruel despot whose uncontrollable anger and hatred of the British were to set in motion a chain of events resulting in two centuries of foreign domination for India.

But he will certainly extol the beauties of the Jain temples, and deservedly so, for they are magnificent. And if, as you wander round this enchanting place, you imagine how once the Maratha Ditch cut right through the gardens, that it was here the Nabob walked alone and made his plans which were to result in the fall of the impregnable city of Calcutta, your daydreams will no doubt be gently interrupted by the melodious voice of the guide, determined to perform his function correctly. Like all good guides, he will tell you in the words of the latest guide-book that Omichand's gardens remain without doubt 'one of the prettiest spots in the whole of Calcutta'.

He will be absolutely right, for nature has a habit of outlasting history.

Brede, East Sussex
January 1963-January 1965

About the Author

NOEL BARBER (1909-88) described himself as "a lad from Doncaster who set out to see the world, not to try and conquer it—heaven forbid—but to enjoy it, to savour it, to work in it, to be a part of it. And to write about it." For more than three decades his adventurous career as a journalist, including long tenure as chief foreign correspondent of London's *Daily Mail*, did indeed allow him to see the world, and his writing about it filled more than twenty books, including history, travel narratives, and best-selling novels.